The Hoola Hoop Paradigm™

The Hoola Hoop Paradigm™

Are You Up for the Challenge? Become as Great as You Want to Be!

Ronald T. Hickey

VelRon

THE HOOLA HOOP PARADIGM™
Are You Up for the Challenge?

For information address Velron Publishing Company, P.O. Box 175, Roseville, CA 95661.

Printed in the United States of America.

10 9 8 7 6 5 4 3 2

ISBN 978-0-61527992-3

Editors: Cathy Orosz, Jo 'Vel Prejean-Hickey, Rochelle Matthews

VelRon Publishing Company
Roseville, California 95661
www.velronpublishing.com

Library of Congress Cataloging-in-Publication Data

Hickey, Ronald Terrence
The hoola hoop paradigm: are you up for the challenge? / Ronald Hickey.—1st ed.
p.cm.
ISBN 978-0-61527992-3 2009923983

Dedication

To my beloved mother Amelia Victoria Robinson for giving me life and for loving me enough to pour your very best into me. I love you Mother Dear!

To my wife Jo' Vel for loving me for who I am and for making this book and everything else I do possible with your patience, understanding, and unconditional love.

To my brilliant, intelligent, and gorgeous children for whom I sacrifice. I love you more than life itself, and you are the very reasons I strive to be as great as I can be. Remember, the blood of Kings and Queens are running through your veins. You must honor this heritage by striving to become great yourself.

To my biological brothers Norris, Robert, and Victor and my spiritual brother Eric, everything you desire of this life is possible. Thank you for your brotherly love.

To the Bakewell, Tennesse gang this book is for you. Your lives have had and continue to have the greatest impact on my life. Your love gave me comfort when I needed it the most. I owe you all. Consider this a down payment.

Contents

Introduction

Are You Up for the Challenge?

"Our deepest fear is not that we are inadequate. Our deepest fear is that we are powerful beyond measure. It is our light, not our darkness, that most frightens us. We ask ourselves, who am I to be brilliant, gorgeous, talented and fabulous? Actually, who are you not to be? You are a child of God. Your playing small does not serve the world. There's nothing enlightened about shrinking so that other people won't feel insecure around you. We were born to make manifest the glory of God that is within us. It's not just in some of us; it's in everyone. And as we let our own light shine, we unconsciously give other people permission to do the same. As we are liberated from our own fear, Our presence automatically liberates others."

—Marianne Williamson

There are two common denominators identifiable with all living species. One, there is an insatiable and incessant desire to succeed in life; and two, all living things are complex creatures and manufactured products of cultural and individual habits. In fact, the milieu of our more successful habits provides profound insight and placid identification of our species. The successful habits of insects identify them as insects and also provide insight as to which type of insect. The successful habits of animals identify them as animals and also provide insight as to which type of animal. Likewise, the habits of humans identify us as humans and also give insight as to what type of human. Our habitual human activities create patterns that differentiate us from other humans. Highly successful people act habitually in manners that identify them both as humans and as highly successful humans. If you were to study the daily activities of any person, you would eventually be able to isolate patterns in that person's life that determine and construct the efficacy in the quality and quantity of his or her existence. There are particular patterns in the life of a man that is a terrific husband and an outstanding father that separates him from men that are not good husbands or good fathers. The success patterns created by a great CEO of a great Fortune 500 company will be majorly different than the success patterns created by a mediocre leader of a mediocre company. There are always particular and very distinctive success patterns in the life of a person that has achieved greatness in his or her life that differentiates him or her from the masses. There are particular and very distinctive success patterns in the life of a woman who has bent the arc of history to become the first female astronaut. There are particular and very distinctive success patterns in the life of a man who has admirably overcome insurmountable odds to become the first African-American President of the United States of America.

The Hoola Hoop Paradigm is a literary work that engages such defined human patterns in a framework of challenges and life principles. The challenges establish a process for personal evaluation of the habitual success activities of others. The challenges provide for the development of new human habits, thus the creation of new life principles to live by. While all humans desire success to a great degree and develop habits to a large degree, we must understand that what works for one does not necessarily work for others, and that old habits are hard to change. It's easy for one to say, "Here are the habits of a highly successful person. Go repeat these habits and you too will be highly successful." But it's not so easy to change your ways and deploy such habits of highly successful people and make them work in your life, despite your determination and drive. If the endeavor was such an easy task, everyone would be a highly successful person. Well, there are definite reasons why a person can't simply take on the habits of others and experience the level of success that others have experienced with the same habits. *The Hoola Hoop Paradigm* explains why success is far more than simply reading about and attempting to repeat the patterns of others.

Imagine being you, and only you, just for a moment. While holding the image of that imagination vividly in your mind, realize that there is only one you and there can be no one else like you. This also means that you can never become anyone else, despite your aspirations. You have your own unique reference when you embark upon any attempt of self-development and self-evaluation. *The Hoola Hoop Paradigm* recognizes your uniqueness and challenges you to become your absolute best. As humans, we are not meant to clone ourselves after others. There will never be another Tiger Woods. There will never be another Bill Gates. There will never be another President Barrack Obama. You have to succeed as you. In your uniqueness, you have established particular patterns in your life. These patterns have provided you with whatever you have and manufactured you into whatever you are. Your level of education, the development of your natural talents and abilities, and your status in life all result from these patterns. To create a better and different you, you have to establish a new set of patterns in your life.

Still, with the image of yourself vividly held in imagination, consider the quality and complexity of the undertaking when you attempt to suppress your mature habits in life while at the same time attempting to create new ones by learning new principles. You have to become a circus act of sorts. In these acts, hoola hoops are the props. During these circus routines, you have to morph into a being that goes from no hoola hoops around your waste to a person that balances and spins multiple hoola hoops around your waste. You have to change how you normally walk and balance your mind and body to ensure you do not drop any of the hoola hoops. This balancing act demonstrates a major shift from your normal human habits. Change does not come easily. Eliminating familiar habits, while implementing new habits simultaneous, is very challenging indeed. To have to implement a sundry of new habits simultaneously presents even greater challenges. *The Hoola Hoop Paradigm* challenges you to do just that. *The Hoola Hoop Paradigm* challenges you to balance and spin a multiplicity of new life principles about your mind, body, and soul as if they were hoola hoops spinning around your waste. And you can not drop either Hoola Hoop Life Principle, without risk to your personal and professional growth.

Developing new life principles requires fervent determination and clear vision. Who you are is both a reference and a challenge to whom and what you desire to become. Our mature human habits tend to exist as the self-imposed limitations to our greater personal and professional development. To change, you must identify and deal with these limitations first. Until you do so, re-creating an all new you is next to impossible and just above delusional. Limitations have this uncanny ability to hold us at bay from where we want to be. The reason for this self-stultification is because we simply refuse to challenge ourselves to understand our limits and create new patterns. Often times, as humans, our limits are simply our own thoughts in reference to ourselves. We don't always believe we are capable of overcoming the obstacles that are staring us in the face. We're not quite sure if we are as brilliant as we say we are. We don't know if we have enough talent. In essence, we don't know who we are. Until you can define unequivocally who you are, you can not seriously consider changes in your life, at least not successful ones. Understanding who you are is one of the hoola hoop principles everyone should have around his or her waist spinning and balanced.

As vibrant and free thinking beings, humans tend to live by varying principles. These sundry of principles, and living as close to these principles as possible, are the primary causes of both the patterns we develop and successes we experience in our lives. For example, if I live by the principle of daily exercise promotes health and longevity in life, subsequently my life will display a pattern of routine physical exercise. A life void of routine exercise underscores a life absent of the principle of health and longevity based on physical exercise. Likewise, a life void of success underscores a life absent the principles required for that success. The basis of *The Hoola Hoop Paradigm* is that there are some core principles in life that must be developed and equally balanced for a person to achieve great levels of success in his or her life. Each principle is likened to a hoola hoop you place around your waist, legs, arms, or some portion of your body. The challenge is to give equal and constant attention to all of your life principles, all of your hoops. The moment you ignore a principle, something stops working in your life. Using the exercise example again, if I ignore the principle that daily exercise promotes health and longevity in life; then my life will not display a pattern of a daily exercise routine, and good health and longevity may not be associated with my life as a result.

Success requires commitment to sound principles and the patterns created. Imagine, if you will, the principles Lance Armstrong must have been committed to and the patterns created in his life when he was riding his way to a record setting seven consecutive championships in cycling. Just imagine the number of hoola hoops he had wrapped around his body that demanded equal and constant attention. In my imagination, I can picture Lance Armstrong giving equal and constant attention to a strict diet, rigid workout routine, mental toughness, strong competitive nature, enormous will to win, and clear vision as principles he was spinning and balancing in his life. To be a champion like Lance Armstrong, whether in your personal life or your professional associations, you must give equal and constant attention to the very principles that will deliver such success. What worked for Lance may not work for you, but there are principles that will work for you. When you are attempting to change your life for the better or desiring to become great at something you are already good at, you may have to add a few more hoola hoops to your daily routine. But you have to look inside yourself to determine the change that must occur. There are no "cookie cutter" patterns for success. You can't simply read about how someone else did it and think all you need to do is pattern your life after the person you just read about. Success is not that simple; even though many works of literature tend to leave you believing it is that easy and simple. *The Hoola Hoop Paradigm* identifies 10 Challenges that will help you develop 10 Life Principles for becoming highly successful. There are no predetermined results. The outcome is determined by both your reference and your input. Your effort will produce an equal reward, but realize that effort alone can not overcome inability. A blind man should not expect to safely land an airplane if effort is all he brings with him to the cockpit. In addition to his efforts, minimally, he will need some knowledge of aviation techniques and a means of understanding the planes position in reference to the runway upon which he wishes to land, since he is blind.

If you accept the challenges in the spirit of, "Success takes time, vision, and determination," you will emerge with 10 new life principles to live by. These principles will become your Hoola Hoop Life Principles. With equal and constant attention afforded to all the new principles, like hoola hoops spinning and balanced around your waist, you will be prepared to succeed in all your life endeavors. You will develop your very own and unique habits and patterns for greatness. When considering the challenges and their transformative effect on your life, imagine each of the challenges as actual hoola hoops that you must spin and balance with your human anatomy. When you can spin and balance the challenges successfully, the challenges are transformed into life principles. Now imagine the 10 new life principles you will develop that you must spin and balance in your life. All the principles must be given equal and constant attention for your life to experience its highest level of success. *The Hoola Hoop Paradigm* was developed on this very principle: *The quality and quantity of one's life is subjugated by one's ability to accept the need to live a life committed to a multiplicity of righteous principles. How well one maintains an equal balance of these powerful and transformative principles will ultimately decide if and to what degree a person succeeds in life.*

THE 10 CHALLENGES and a brief note on the life principles associated with each are as follows:

CHALLENGE 1: DISCOVER WHO YOU ARE

Self-discovery is real power in learning to become the best person possible. Whether in a personal relationship; a position as a sole source contributor, team player and team leader, CEO, or home maker; understanding your abilities, limitations, vision, and brilliance is paramount to optimizing your influence on success. Lack of self-knowledge limits your ability to determine your individual ambitions and how you can best serve yourself and others. Knowledge gives you information. Information can be shared. If there is no pertinent information you can share with others about yourself, you may want to re-assess your ability to support the goals of the team, whether that team is your family, your co-workers, or your friends. Your life principles, those deep beliefs that govern your life, have to align with the vision of the team for you to be of positive contributor to the team's vision and goals. But you must know exactly who you are before that assessment can be made. Self-discovery is the very first step to obtaining directions for your successful life. You can not properly map-out the journey toward high achievement if you don't know the starting point. Who you are is your starting point. Who you are determines if you have what it takes to complete the journey. Who you are determines if you bring enough to the cockpit to safely land the airplane.

Challenge 2: Clearly Identify Your Ambitions

Ambitions create a strong desire to achieve something. Sharing ambitions between individuals and groups of individuals helps establish an atmosphere for trusting teamwork and achieving success. Marriages are more successful when ambitions are shared between spouses. Organizations are more successful when ambitions are shared in the boardroom. Teams win championships when teammates share a common ambition. Ambition allows everyone the ability to determine if there is a common purpose within the family, organization, or team that is in complete alignment with the ambitions of the individuals and the overall vision of the group or partnership. In essence, identifying ambitions determines if there truly is a cause to struggle for. Spouses must share their ambitions with their partners in a marriage, and the two must have common ambitions for the marriage to be successful. Teammates must have a common goal and a common interest in reaching the goal to be successful as a team. Businesses succeed only if everyone shares a common desire to achieve. Clearly identifying your ambitions will determine if you are on the right team to succeed.

Challenge 3: Properly Align and Manage Your Talents for Success

Understanding your innate abilities and natural talents and the abilities and talents of individuals on the team is vitally important to ensuring you have the ability to properly align talent for peak performance. If you are unequivocally aware of the talent pool, you can best deploy your resources for optimum achievement. Understanding the depths of your ability also allows you to identify weakness in the talent pool. This knowledge is as important to success as knowing your strengths. In addition, proper management of talent (ensuring every individual is tasked and rewarded in a manner that supports their individual ambitions and the ambitions of the team) is the sure way to talent retention and recruitment. Everyone wants to feel that their skills are recognized, utilized, and appreciated. Proper talent alignment results in self-actualization. Self-actualization is the ultimate in personal satisfaction and the true measure of self-worth.

CHALLENGE 4: CREATE A FRAMEWORK FOR CRITICAL THINKING

Critical thinking will produce new perceptions and new ideas. Perception defines your vision and desire for something. Perceptions generate all our thoughts and feelings. Ideas motivate us to action. With new perceptions and fresh ideas, we step in the direction of success and unprecedented achievement. Furthermore, and perhaps most importantly, a solid framework for critical thinking eliminates the dependency on others to solve your every problem. If an organization is constantly employing outside consultants to come in and figure out what is wrong, then the organization also needs to re-assess its talent pool for adequacy and weakness. Marriage counseling should never be an acceptable substitute for developing the ability to solve your own marital problems. Conflict resolution, change management, peak performance, and team building should never result in costly consultant fees. Everyone needs to develop the ability to think creatively and critically to bring resolve to their own issues.

CHALLENGE 5: DEVELOP PROCESS PATTERNS FOR SUCCESS

Process patterns can ensure you are either consistently successful or consistently unsuccessful. The goal should be to develop process patterns that are proven to deliver success. Failure will simply happen from time to time, no process pattern can guarantee peak performance 100% of the time. But proven patterns will increase your success rate to a predictable level. Process patterns, not individual errors or successes, are the keys to a successful journey. The goal in developing patterns is to ensure you are not carrying errors forward and your process delivers desired results each and every time. Additionally, process patterns will negate weaknesses in your talent pool. Allow great process patterns to be the architect of your business and operational strategies and performance will reach levels well beyond your current abilities. Happy and healthy relationships require successful process patterns as well. Happiness does not happen by accident. You must develop habits that result in the conditions you want in your life.

CHALLENGE 6: UNDERSTAND WHAT WORKS AND WHY IT WORKS

Once process patterns are developed that deliver desired results each and every time, you should study initially on the reasons the patterns are successful or effective. You can eliminate mistakes by sticking to what you fully understand. Focusing on what you know provides an atmosphere of confidence in your work and promotes a foundation for growth. You can not get better at something until you understand what you are doing right and why you are doing it right. Without understanding this, success is only a matter of luck; and failure is simply a matter of time.

CHALLENGE 7: UNDERSTAND WHAT DOES NOT WORK AND WHY IT DOES NOT WORK

Understand what patterns are not working and why they are not working. Positive continuous growth, quarter after quarter and year after year, cannot take place until obstacles to successful pattern developing are eliminated. Understanding what does not work and why it does not work will also prevent carrying errors forward. Failure to understand what does not work and why it does not work are the very reasons organizations waste time, resources, and energy trying to get different results with the same old process. Albert Einstein once stated that, *"The definition of insanity is doing the same thing over and over, but expecting different results."* Organizational insanity is the result of not understanding why something does not work, so you keep doing it regardless. Many of us are guilty of this in our personal relationships as well.

CHALLENGE 8: TRUST IN YOUR OWN ABILITIES

If you can not trust your own abilities, or the abilities of your teammates, to think critically to bring resolve to fundamental problems in your process patterns, you will never reach your full potential and your team will never experience the success that only comes from interdependency. There are only a few things that are more appalling within a teamwork atmosphere than a person who does not trust his or her teammates. Have you ever noticed the difference in NBA Superstars Allen Iverson, Kobe Bryant or Paul Pierce when they play with teammates they trust, as opposed to teammates they do not trust? Just like NBA Superstars, if you trust your teammates; your individual statistics may decrease, but the team's success rate increases. And vice versa, if you do not trust your teammates; your individual statistics may increase, but the team's success rate decreases. Trusting in the abilities of your teammates is synonymous with a high success rate of any team and any organization.

CHALLENGE 9: LEARN FROM YOUR EXPERIENCES

Any process must be examined. Experience allows learning from execution of the process. Grade the process fairly, and trust the process based on the grade. Learn from both your mistakes and your successes. Mastering this challenge is paramount for developing trust in your abilities and the abilities of your teammates. If you can not examine and grade your own work, then it becomes essentially impossible to establish the degree of your abilities in reference to the full potential of the process. Socrates once stated that,

"The unexamined life was not worth living." In an organizational setting, the unexamined process is worthless to your business. You simply must learn from your experiences, successes and failures. If you fail to do so, you are just going through the motions; like so many are doing in their personal relationships and businesses.

CHALLENGE 10: UNDERSTAND THAT GREATNESS HAS TO BE COACHED

Every individual and organization should instinctively understand that talent alone will not harness success, no matter the level of ambition and talent. Every great team has a great coach that coaches the great ambitions and talents of the individuals on the team to success and championships. This fact has always been and will always be true. Even the world's greatest golfer, Tiger Woods, with all of his talent and ambition has a swing coach. If Tiger Woods understands that he needs a great coach so he can be great in the sport of golf, shouldn't all organizations and every person embrace the fact that you need a great coach if you are to be great in business and life?

Each of the above challenges is thoroughly discussed in detail within chapters of the book. The impending principles of each challenge are illuminated so each individual can evaluate the value of each principle in his or her life. No two individuals will derive at the exact same conclusion. This is not a book designed to be a "one-size-fits-all" type of read. As stated earlier, your reward will equal your effort. *Are You Up for the Challenge?* The 10 Challenges will provide you the necessary insight into your own psyche and an understanding of just how powerful your God given talents, personal ambitions and passionate visions truly are. You will embrace the fact that you have the mental toughness to accept challenges and emerge a better, more improved wife, husband, brother, sister, co-worker, father, mother, employee, leader, or teammate. You will learn that properly aligning your talents, ambitions and passions will deliver you to any level of greatness that you dare to set your sights on. This book will assist you in self-liberating the anecdote of your life, which is one of the very reasons we walk this earth. If you accept the 10 challenges, and I know you will, you will overcome your self-imposed limits; and you shall be liberated from your own fears. You will emerge with new principles that will forever connect you to the idea that you are as brilliant, gorgeous, talented and fabulous as anyone who has ever lived. Your life is your life, no one else's. Your walk is your walk, no one else's. Your success is your success, no one else's. What you become will be determined by who you are right now and by the new habits you develop, starting today.

As you accept these 10 challenges and journey down the path to greatness, understand that many obstacles will present themselves along the way. Life is not, nor is it designed to be, trouble free. But also understand that you are everything you think you are and so much more. You are a child of God, and you are to manifest His greatness by becoming great yourself. Don't play yourself small. As Tiger Woods would tell you, always bring your "A" game. Your "A" game will give others permission to bring their "A" games as well, and everyone will shine. Never shrink yourself for any reason. No one or no situation will ever benefit from you being small. As other challenges come your way, accept them with boldness and intrepidness; for your challenges are the measuring rods that will determine just how great you become. Success and greatness is not measured by how far you travel in life, but rather by what you had to overcome to get there. Whatever your agenda may be, if you are truly up to the challenges of life, this book will assist you in creating the absolute best personal and professional life your natural talents, creative imagination, passions, energy, ambitions, and knowledge can deliver. You are only limited by your unwillingness to accept the challenges before you. Understand that the universe is ready for you to become whomever you decide to be. And the universe is not limited by your limitations. The universe is not limited by your lack of education, impoverished upbringing, or mental and physical impediments. God's greatness and power will be manifested in your life as soon as you decide to straddle the spirit of ambition and ride through, over, under or around every obstacle standing in your way. Your ambitions establish your limits more than any other aspect of your life. With ambition, you can overcome under-education. With ambition, you can conquer under-achievement. With ambition, you can become the next great CEO, author, doctor, politician, talk show host, national news anchor, and everything else you want to be, even President of the United States. *Are you up for the challenge?*

I fully understand that there are many works of literature on the market with similar subjects. So I appreciate the opportunity to impart unto you my fresh ideas. As my pastor would say, "I have attempted to draw fresh water from an old well." I am certain that this book and the new strategies discussed within will make a magnificent difference in your life if you commit to applying the knowledge to your situation(s). I know they have made and continue to make all the difference in both my personal and professional lives. I suggest you read the book in its entirety, without working on any of the challenges, the first time through. Then read the book again. During the second read, accept one challenge at a time. Conquer the challenges in sequence for the greatest effect on the quality and quantity of your life. Attempting to conquer the challenges all at once will send your life into overload, and that will be counterproductive to achieving the level of greatness you have set your sights on. Start with small goals and allow the attainment of the small goals to assist you in the development of confidence in the process. Take on larger goals once you have established your own proven process patterns. Your whole life depends on you becoming as great as you want to be, and the journey is definitely a marathon. But just like training for a marathon, you slowly build up to running 26 miles. If you attempt to run 26 miles the first day of training, you will overwhelm yourself and vacate the entire process. As you methodically work through the challenges, remember the idea is to incite yourself from within. The universe has already given you all that you require to be as great as you want to be. You simply need to unblock the pathways of your passions and allow those passions to merge with the universe so they can intersect with your talents and ambitions. Combined, they will take you to the far reaches of the universe and back; and everyone will know your name. I can hardly wait to meet you. I know you are as excited as I am. So, let's get started!

CHALLENGE ONE

DISCOVER WHO YOU ARE

"Be brave enough to live life creatively. The creative is the place where no one else has ever been. You have to leave the city of your comfort and go into the wilderness of your intuition. You can't get there by bus, only hard work and risk and by not quite knowing what you are doing. What you'll discover will be wonderful. What you'll discover will be yourself."

—Alan Alda

Our natural talents and abilities are creation designed. God ensures that our capabilities as humans are a congener to his divine calling for our lives. Once you discover who you are, you will instinctively understand what you have been called to do. A world renowned opera singer is born with such a magnificent voice that his or her natural talents and abilities are revealed very early in life. The opera singer simply has to discover his self or herself to understand his or her calling. What you are here to accomplish becomes so crystal clear once you are able to match your innate gifts with your true calling. In her book, *Life's a Journey, Not a Sprint,* my friend Jennifer Lewis-Hall states, *"We need to pay attention to what really moves us in life. That's how I discovered that I was passionate about journalism and would most likely succeed if I chose it as a career. I was always a people person, wanting to know more about individuals and their stories. While many find it nerve-racking, after my "Uncle Sam" speech in high school, I realized that I felt comfortable speaking in front of an audience. And despite the intense competition involved in breaking into journalism, I always believed in my soul that it was the right career for me."* You have to understand your ambitions and your talents, and you have to find your passion; that thing that calls you so loud that you can't ignore it. Once you discover who you are and conjoin that knowledge with your purpose, ambitions, and passion; you will experience success in mastodonic proportion and degree.

Discovering and understanding who you are is absolutely necessary if you have any desire to reach your full unbridled potential because the knowledge of self establishes the reference point from which all of your travels begin. If you do not know where you are in your life, then you can not sense the directions for where you want to go in your life. Likewise, if you have no sense of who you are, in terms of your innate talents, personal ambitions and passions in life; then you will not have the ability to map out the directions for who you think you want to become or for what you think you want to do with your life. Here is a practical illustration: If you log on to the internet and logon to the Yahoo or Google website to access a Map Quest search engine, the first bit of information the Map Quest search engines asks for is your starting point. If you do not know your starting point, the search engines will not allow you to simply enter a destination and obtain accurate directions. You have to enter a starting address and a destination address. At that point the search engines will provide you with clear directions for your travels, as long as both points are recognizable addresses.

Your personal and professional lives operate in an identical manner. You can not simply say you want to become an astronaut or CEO of the company and then ask the universe for accurate directions. You can not simply say you want to become an impassioned artist in your spare time or a world-renowned author and motivational speaker and then ask the universe for accurate directions. You have to first understand if you have been blessed with the innate talents and abilities to become an astronaut, CEO, impassioned artist or author. You then have to understand if you have the ambition and passion to combine with your talents. Who you are currently determines the directions you must travel to become the person you so strongly desire to become. Who you are determines if the journey is even possible. Being an author has associated educational pre-requisites. Do you have the required imagination and subject matter expertise to become a great author and or a motivational speaker? Becoming an astronaut requires you to possess certain physical and mental abilities. Do you possess such abilities? Neil Alden Armstrong was an American astronaut, test pilot, university professor, and United States Naval Aviator. He is the first person to set foot on the Moon. His first spaceflight was aboard Gemini 8 in 1966, for which he was the command pilot. On this mission, he helped performed the first manned docking of two spacecrafts. Neil Armstrong's second and also his last spaceflight was as mission commander of the Apollo 11 moon landing mission on July 20, 1969. Mr. Armstrong is a recipient of the Congressional Space Medal of Honor. Before becoming an astronaut, Neil Armstrong was in the United States Navy and saw action in the Korean War. After the war, he served as a test pilot at the National Advisory Committee for Aeronautics (NACA) High-Speed Flight Station, now known as the Dryden Flight Research Center, where he flew over 900 flights in a variety of aircraft. As a research pilot, Armstrong served as project pilot on the F-100 Super Sabre A and C aircraft, F-101 Voodoo, and the Lockheed F-104A Starfighter. He also flew the Bell X-1B, Bell X-5, North American X-15, F-105 Thunderchief, F-106 Delta Dart, B-47 Stratojet, KC-135 Stratotanker and Paresev. He graduated from Purdue University. Neil Armstrong was not the average every day person. He, like all astronauts, possessed some specific talents, ambitions, and visions for becoming such a great American. An artist has to have a creative imagination, ambition, and vision for becoming a great artist. Just consider all the attributes that made Monet such a great artist. Do you possess such attributes? Do you have such an imagination, ambition and vision as Monet? Becoming a CEO of a company requires a plethora of professional attributes. Consider everything Jack Welch needed to become such an iconic CEO. Are you the next Jack Welch? Do you meet those requirements? In all circumstances, knowing who and where you are determines the direction you must travel to become who you desire to be or get to where you desire to go. Whether you desire to be the next Neil Armstrong, great artist, or the next CEO of a great company, you have to have the talent, ambition, and vision for what you desire to become. But just like performing a search on one of the internet search engines, you have to enter the information that establishes where you are in life before you can obtain accurate directions for where you want to go.

My mother always taught me to never forget where I came from. She always said, "You can always come back home if things don't work out in one place and you need to get a fresh start in life." Knowing where you came from means you are never lost. You can always get back to your reference point. No matter where I am in the world, I can always get back home. I always know how to get back to Chattanooga, Tennessee. I am never lost because I always know where I came from. In your place of employment, in a team environment, knowledge of self-awareness is so important as well. Know who you are. Understand your talents, ambitions and passions. Constantly assess if your needs compliment the needs of the organization. Don't be afraid to answer honestly when the answer is "no." If the answer is "no" travel back to where you came from. Get back to the basics. Do not work in a position where you can not fully satisfy the needs of the team and the team can not fully satisfy your needs. Play to your strengths. When Michael Jordan left the NBA for a career in Major League Baseball, he had the passion and ambition for the game; but he did not have the talent. He elected to give up his try at baseball because he understood that baseball could not satisfy his need to succeed at the same level at which he succeeded in the NBA. He understood that his talent level did not satisfy the needs of his team. Michael returned to the NBA. He knew his way home. He had a sense of direction in his life because he understood who and where he was and understood who and where he wanted to be as an athlete. We all need to become more efficient at making similar assessments in our personal and professional lives. Far too many of us are not talented enough, or ambitious enough or passionate enough in our lives. As a result, our team is suffering because we fail to meet the needs of the team. Work should never be only about the paycheck if you expect any degree of job satisfaction or personal happiness.

Years ago, I was hired as a portfolio manager at a collections agency. On the first day of employment, the owner of the company entered the orientation class and spoke to the group of us that had just been hired. He made a comment during his monologue that has made an impact in my life ever since. Mr. Phillips described how he had failed at many things in his life until he discovered that he had a talent and passion for the collections business. He was very ambitious about his newly discovered talent and passion and decided to start his own collections agency. Ten years later, and millions of dollars in revenue later, Mr. Phillips was standing before the group of us addressing his newly hired employees. He challenged each and every one of us. He said ask yourself if you have an innate passion and natural talent for the collections business. Mr. Phillips said, if you do not have passion and talent, you will never develop into an ambitious employee. He said that success in the business would be mediocre at best without talent, passion and ambition. Mr. Phillips went further and stated that the collections business is not the business to work in just to make a paycheck. I thought seriously about what my new boss has just said. I embraced the challenge he had just laid out before me. At the first break of the orientation class, I went to the Personnel Department and informed the Personnel Director that I no longer had any interest in employment with the company, and I left the building immediately. I was a portfolio manager at a collections agency for only two hours. That was my shortest tenure in employment at any company. I knew this type of employment was not the situation in which my talents and passions would be fully deployed. Since that brief job, I have never again applied for or accepted a job that did not compliment who I was, my talent, ambition and passion. As a result, I have been highly successful at all of my places of employment. If you find that you are not or have not been successful in your employment, perhaps you need to discover just who you are and assess if your employment choice compliments your talent, ambition and passion. You may be engaged in an endeavor that has no potential for success and happiness for you.

Each of your life teams; whether the team is your family, friends, co-workers, association members, or sports teammates, will need you at your absolute best for the sake of the success of the team. One of the most important things in life is to challenge yourself beyond your comfort zones. Your reach should extend well beyond what is easily in your grasp. When you challenge yourself in such a manner you began to forge the pathways that lead to your full potential. You can not truly and fairly challenge yourself until you know exactly who you are. Self-awareness will limit the risk of disenfranchising yourself from the entire success process. An armless man should understand that he is not likely to succeed as a NASCAR Indy 500 racecar driver.

So here is the first challenge: Discover who you are before you do anything else in or with your life, at home or at work. Sit down with a pen and notebook, or at your computer and do the following: I suggest that you use a notebook that is of a very high quality, perhaps leather bound. The paper should be of equal quality. Also select the most expensive pen you can afford. This project will be a reflection of your life. Place a value on your life right now and let that value reflect in the quality of this project. You should be of the mindset that you are about to write a book about your most valuable treasure: your life.

THE FIRST CHALLENGE:

- Write down everything you know about yourself.
- List your ambitions (every one).
- List your passions (every one).
- Write down your current vision for your life.
- Write down your vision for your life 5 years from now.
- Write down your vision for your life 10 years from now.
- Write down your vision for your life in retirement.
- List all of your God-given talents.
- Write down three things about yourself that you have never shared.
- Write down your likes and dislikes.
- Write down your favorite subjects in high school and/or college.
- List every thing you have ever aspired to be.
- If you had three wishes, list what you would wish for and why.
- How would you choose to live if you had only six months to live?

- If today was your last day on earth, describe the entire last 24 hours of your life.

- What has been your greatest joy in life?

- Write down what has been your greatest regret in life.

- Write down what has been your greatest regret as a professional.

- List all your failures.

- List all your triumphs.

- List everything you know you are good at.

- List everything you know you are bad at.

- Write down each of your most rewarding professional accomplishments.

- Write down each of your most rewarding personal accomplishments.

- List everything you can not live without.

- List the things in your life that you do not need.

- List everything you like about your current job and co-workers.

- List everything you dislike about your current job and co-workers.

- Write down everything you are afraid of.

- List three individuals you most admire and why.

- List every person you dislike and why.

- List your fantasies.

- List everything you believe you are capable of doing, but never had the chance to try.

- Write down the names of every important person in your life.

- List the three people you want to meet in Heaven and why.

- Write down your fondest childhood memory.

- Write the story of the worst time of your life.

- List three things do you like the most about yourself?

- List three things do you like the least about yourself?

- Describe a perfect day in your life?

- Write your obituary as if your life reached its zenith today.

- List three things that are worth dying for.

- List your top 5 priorities in life.

- Write your epitaph as you want it to read on your grave stone.

- Write a letter to your unborn great grandchildrento tell them what no one else will be able to tell them about you.

"When you discover who you are, you'll be free."

—Ralph Emerson

Now that you are beginning to develop an idea of who you are, do the following the very next day after you have completed the tasks above:

- Describe your values in life.

- Describe your belief system.

- List five changes you would make in your life if you could today.

- Of the five changes you list, commit to making one of those changes today. Then commit to making the remaining changes by years end. Remember, the choice is truly yours.

I know this is a difficult and challenging list. Self-discovery can be a challenging and complex endeavor. Many of the items you have answered in the above exercises may represent questions you have never asked yourself. Some of the answers are down right painful to contemplate. Malcolm X once said, *"The examined life is painful."* Avoiding the pain is why so many of us are walking around not knowing who we truly are. This lack of self-knowledge is why so many of us are in unsatisfying situations at our places of employment and at home in our personal relationships. Our talents and abilities are misaligned, and we have blocked ourselves from finding our passion and pathways for success. We have settled in jobs simply because the job pays the bills. We are in relationships that badly need to end because we don't have the esteem to start over. We are on teams that are marred in destitute situations because no one has a reference for the direction the team needs to travel. If you approach the above exercise in a serious manner, and if you are willing to be honest with yourself, you will find yourself in the *"wilderness of your intuition"* that Alan Alda speaks of. In that wilderness is exactly where you will discover yourself. Review and edit all of your answers every single day for one month. I assure you, you will discover you in the process.

By no stretch of the imagination are the questions above suggested as the only questions or process to self-discovery. My hope is that this simply starts a dialogue with yourself that will last a lifetime. My hope is that you avoid what Moses experienced when he freed the Israelites. After Moses freed the slaves, the Christian Bible informs us that they wandered in the wilderness for forty years. When they finally made it to the promised-land that Moses had spoken of so fervently of for forty years, they realized that every day for those forty years they had been only an eight days travel from their destination. The freed slaves, once free, began to distrust Moses and others, despite trusting Moses enough to be led out of bondage. The Israelites forgot who they were as a people. They did not know who they were as individuals. The road map was unclear. They lost their way. So for forty years, they remained eight days from there destination. In your life, do you trust the road map to success, happiness, and the promised-land? Has the way been lost to find joy in your personal relationships or professional assertions? Have you been wandering forty years in your life when the destination is only eight days away? Self-discovery will put you back on the right path. Self-discovery will allow you to trust in yourself and in others. And a commitment to a lifetime of personal dialogue with yourself will ensure that the way is always directly ahead of you. Develop your own questions and processes for learning more and more about yourself. There is no one book that is a summation of your gorgeous and brilliant life. There is no one list of specific questions and answers that will ever identify everything concerning your complicated and precious life. You have to self-liberate the anecdote for yourself.

Enlightened with the basic intimate knowledge of yourself, you are now ready to start the journey to becoming your absolute best. Realize this is not the end, but the beginning of self-awareness. You have spent your entire life standing at bay from your true self wandering in the wilderness of your existence. Therefore, a journey is necessary to get to the promise land of where life is lived deliberately. In this promised land of the self-enlightened you, your teammates will start to understand you more because you will be able to assist them in their understanding. Your spouse, children, parents, siblings, friends, acquaintances, and colleagues will start to understand you more because you will be able to assist them in understanding you. But most of all, you will understand yourself. You will be prepared to recognize if your talents and abilities align with your ambitions and passions. You will have a reference point for your life. You will then be able to logon to your virtual universe and access the search engine of your purpose and enter your starting point, and get accurate directions to your desired destination. You will have discovered who you are, and you will be free. That's exactly where you want to be.

"If, at age 50, I thought and believed as I did when I was 20 years old; I would have just wasted 30 years of my life."

—Muhammad Ali

Your life should involve you constantly striving to better yourself, and maturity should bring about change in how you think and in what you believe. Who you are should only be a reference point in your life, never the mark of your final destination. Your life should be like a map of the globe, and your goal should be to travel every square inch of the globe. If you have not operated in such a manner, then you have possibly wasted some years of your life. But now that you have discovered who you are and now that you are free, its time to make some fresh decisions about who you want to be and what you want to do with your life. If you are like most people, currently you are not who you want to be, and therefore you are not doing what you want to do with your life. This is the source of our unhappiness at home and at work. Your life is out of alignment. Your desires, talents, ambitions, passions and visions are in complete misalignment of one another. Discover you. This knowledge will give you that very important reference point in your life. The knowledge of self allows you to determine where you are in life so you can ask yourself if where you are is where you want to be. Most of us don't have the personal and professional lives that we really and truly want. That means we are not the best father, mother, son, daughter, husband, wife, friend, colleague, employee, teammate or person for any of the positions we may currently occupy. Becoming a better you and becoming as great as you want to be is about the alignment of your current self with your future self. And you have to be able to draw a line and connect those two points of reference if the journey is to be successful. Without that connecting line, you waste years wandering in the wilderness of your illusions, your illusions of who and where you are.

As a professional at your place of employment, ask yourself if your current employer can provide a situation and workplace environment that provides for you drawing a connecting line between your current life and your desired future life of unprecedented success and high achievement. Remember, you have already discovered who you are, and you are free to be whomever you choose to be. The process of self-discovery is not the finish line; it's the starting gate. So, again, ask yourself if your current employment allows a line of travel to where and who you want to be as a professional. If the answer is yes, then you should work on developing relationships and mentorships within your company that will allow you to connect the line of travel between your two reference points, point A and point B, current position and future position. If the answer is no, then you need to get very busy finding employment with another organization. Do yourself and your current company a large favor, and do not work there one more day longer than what is absolutely necessary. You will never become self-actualized in an organization that does not provide you with a clear path to your desired level of professional achievement within the organization. You will never experience any degree of sustained happiness with your current employment if your talents and passions are under utilized and unrewarded. Recognize that self-actualization is a basic human need. Even the greatest among us desires complete satisfaction with and self-actualization in his or her life.

The pathways to greatness are inundated with many challenges along the way. The weary travelers of the pathways to success and high achievement must be wise enough to understand that candidates for greatness must be subjected to a series of rigorous tests to determine their worthiness for the prize. In the spirit of wisdom and challenge, we must assess our own abilities and worthiness to advance on the path to greatness. We are not acting with wisdom when we accept challenges and endeavors we know we are not prepared for. To do so knowing we are not up to the challenge or qualified for the task at hand is the equivalent to accepting an invitation for failure. Knowledge of who you are will determine your ability to conquer the challenges along your current path to success and examine your qualifications to occupy the space you seek. Ponder seriously who you are. If you are not the right person for the job, don't accept the job. Don't accept invitations for failure. If you fail enough times, you will convince yourself that you are incapable of accomplishing anything. You will find yourself incarcerated in a prison of fear. Your fear will control you to the ends of the earth. Your personal life will falter. Your professional life will be mediocre at best. Every team you are associated with will have limited success. On the other hand, if you are the right person for the job; your talents, ambitions, and passions align with the vision of the position you occupy; your personal life will be as great as you want it to be. Your professional life will be as great as you want it to be. Every team you are associated with will receive maximum benefits from your contributions.

"Direct your eye sight inward, and you'll find a thousand regions in your mind yet undiscovered. Travel them and be expert on home cosmography."

—Henry David Thoreau

Life has a precious gift for each of us. This precious gift is wrapped in the finest of tapestry. That tapestry is self-awareness. Once you unwrap that knowledge of who you are, the precious gift of your life will be revealed, not just to you but also to the world. Your gift should be treasured; for God placed the very best of everything into you. For that reason, at work and at play, in joy and in sadness, in your profession and in your personal life, in a regular season game and in the title game, in your aspirations and in your challenges, in your defeats and in your triumphs, in your pain and in your comfort; seek nothing short of absolute greatness. And the very first step in the process of discovering your life's precious gift is discovering the complete and unequivocal knowledge of who you are. If you fail to take this first step, any other steps will be out of order. So, order your steps. Accept the challenge to discover who you are, and just as important, demand that others accept the challenge to discover who they are as well. You will be hard pressed to identify any situation where you will benefit from being the only one enlightened with self-knowledge. Everyone you intend to engage in a long-term mutual relationship of any sort should be just as prepared to introduce his self or herself to you as you are prepared to introduce yourself to him or her, if the relationship is to flourish.

In a team setting, developing trust becomes very challenging when team players have no knowledge of who their teammates are. Most individuals and organizations understand this concept as a universal truth. That is why many companies spend thousands of dollars; some may spend even millions, on team building exercises, workshops, seminars and even retreats for top executives. The problem, more often than not, with all of these team building activities is that very few in attendance are enlightened with self-awareness. Without self-awareness among the attendees, not much trust can be developed among the team members. Without trust, how much team building can truly be accomplished? Even in this information age, everyone continues to hesitate when it comes to sharing information about his self or herself. Is this because we are private individuals or simply shy by nature? Or is this because we know very little about ourselves, thus we don't know what to share. Whatever the case may be, the environment for team building is placed at a grave disadvantage when self-awareness remains a fleeting thought. This includes our personal lives, where trust is most important. Stop for a minute and imagine, if you will, that your spouse, friend, co-worker, supervisor or another member of a board that you sat on comes up to you and asks you to describe who you are. How would you answer? Would your answer be the first step in building trust? If so, what information would you share in the future to ensure that complete trust is developed? This leads to the next exercise in discovering who you are.

Based on the information you provided in the initial exercise in this chapter, after reviewing and editing the information each day for a month, answer the following questions:

- Your spouse asks, who are you?

- Your best friend asks, who are you?

- A colleague asks, who are you?

- Your current boss asks, who are you?

- A teammate on your sports team asks, who are you?

- A student in your class asks, who are you?

Are your answers different based on the person asking? If the answers are different based on the individual asking, why is that so? Do your answers develop trust, or identify areas of distrust, between you and the individuals? Introduce yourself to you. Answer yourself, as if you were asking yourself, "Who are you?" Self-discovery is real power in determining your individual ambitions and how you can best serve on the team, at home and at work. Knowledge gives you information. Information can be shared. If there is no pertinent information you can share with your team, at home or at work, about yourself, you may want to re-assess your ability to support the goals of the team. Something about you (talents, ambitions, and visions) has to align with the vision of the team for you to be of positive assistance to the team. Self-discovery is very critical to leadership and teamwork environments.

As you go forth, discovered and free, expend a tremendous amount of energy in providing self-care to yourself. Develop a maintenance program that assists you in remaining completely self-aware because your beliefs and values should and will change over time. Exercise your body, eat a careful diet, and feed your spirit through personal relationships and prayer on a daily basis. Engage in dialogue with yourself weekly. When you give such personal attention to yourself, you energize and incite yourself to serve others. When you know you have taken care of yourself, you are free to be less self-centered and more other-people centered and serve mankind in a manner that will be nothing short of amazing. At that very point you will exists as the perfect steward to yourself and ambassador to the world. Discovered and free, is the first step in becoming as great as you want to be.

Are you ready to become as great as you want to be? Are you up for the next challenge? If so, let's go share your ambitions with those who are a part of your personal and professional lives.

Challenge Two

Clearly Identify Your Ambitions

"To become great requires ambition. Birthright may make you a King, but only ambition can make you a Great King. Ambition raises us above ourselves; above our failures, above our obstacles, and above our limits."

—Ronald T. Hickey

Ambition creates a strong desire to achieve something special. An individual must harness great ambition if he or she is to achieve great success. To have a wonderful marriage, a couple must possess an ambition congenial to producing such a relationship. Teams, like two individuals in a marriage, are formed for the purpose of achieving something they are not able to as individuals. So teams must have great ambition if they are to become great teams. And everyone on the team must identify his or her ambitions. You must know your ambitions and the ambitions of everyone on your team. Those collective ambitions must be in proper alignment. In a business relationship, a partnership can not survive if one partner desires fervently to become a great producer of a particular product and the other has only a high aspiration of making money. The ambition to get rich is not necessarily properly aligned with the ambition of building a great product. John D. Rockefeller expressed, *"The person who starts out simply with the idea of getting rich won't succeed; you must have a larger ambition. There is no mystery in business. If you do each day's task successfully, and stay faithfully within these natural operations of commercial laws which I talk so much about, and keep your head clear, you will come out all right."* I think everyone would agree that John D. Rockefeller came out all right. Mr. Rockefeller also shared his ambitions with his team. His teammates shared their ambitions with Mr. Rockefeller. Their collective ambitions were properly aligned, as a result, the founder of Exxon Oil, Mr. John D. Rockefeller did more than just come out all right; he became mastodonic as a business man. Sharing ambitions between the team leader and the team players helps establish an atmosphere for trusting teamwork and achieving success. This charity also allows the team to assess if there is a common purpose amongst the team that is in complete alignment with the ambitions of the individuals and the visions of the organization. In essence, identifying ambitions determines if there truly is a team. Teammates must have a common goal and a common interest in reaching the goal to be successful as a team.

Sharing your ambitions with others involves being completely honest about yourself and your goals in life. The first and previous chapter discussed the importance of discovering who you are. Self-discovery unlocks the mysteries of what you truly desire to do with your life. You are not placing a high value on your true self if your actions support a prevarication of your true ambitions. You have to have the courage and willingness to be honest about who you are as a person and about what you truly desire to become or accomplish in this human existence. You do yourself and others a disservice when you play yourself small. Don't play yourself small. You play yourself small when you are not openly honest about your true desires and values in life. Let everyone know; your spouse, co-workers, boss, friends, siblings, children, business partners, or others in your associations, that something inside you vehemently motivates you to strive for high achievements and great successes. Let everyone know you have big dreams and you plan to devote your life to fulfilling those big dreams. If others on your team, in your personal relationships, or in your work environment fail to share your ambitions, do not support the falsehood that the endeavor will be successful, despite the misalignment of ambitions. Without a common ambition, or at least complimenting ambitions; teammates will be hard pressed to identify common goals and interests. Without those common goals and interests, I believe success to any degree is next to impossible. If you and your spouse have competing ambitions that fail to provide for any common goals or interests, then you will inevitably develop a very horrid resentment for your spouse, and your relationship will never blossom into anything special. More than likely, the relationship will experience an unhealthy demise because there is no common interest upon which to focus your efforts, thus you will simply grow apart. Likewise, if you and your teammates, at work or at play, have misaligned ambitions that fail to produce common goals and interests, then you will create an atmosphere rot with low morale, discord and dissention within the team. Such an atmosphere is not suitable for providing an opportunity for success. If such conditions exist, and circumstances allow, you should end your association with the team.

While finding another team can be the appropriate thing to do, simply changing geography very seldom solves the problem. After a while you discover that similar issues exist in the new situation. One of the problems with leaving one team for other, whether in personal relationships or professional settings, is you more often than not fail to understand the reasons you were not successful on the last team. You bring your old baggage into a new set of circumstances. You are clueless to the fact that not identifying and sharing your ambitions and the ambitions of others is the primary reason you find yourself in unwinnable, unreasonable, improper, and unhealthy situations, conditions, and environments. You must discuss ambitions and vision in detail with your spouse if you desire a special relationship with your mate. Each person must fully understand the goals and aspirations of the other. The partnership must produce common interests that simultaneously support the desires of the individuals, and the individual desires must compliment each other. There is an old Hungarian saying that a Hungarian friend of mine shared with me that states, *"You can't ride two horses with one ass."* In partnerships, there must be one vision shared by all. Two people must be in concert with one another to be successful. A husband and wife, joined as one, can not chase separate dreams that do not provide a common thread for weaving the fabric of a great marriage. Teammates must share a common goal of winning championships if they expect to be successful. Teams simply have to have a common interest that is shared by each and every person. Partnerships can not succeed with everyone doing their own thing and promoting their individual self-interests.

"Keep away from people who try to belittle your ambitions. Small people do that, but the really great make you feel that you, too, can become great."

—Mark Twain

Great relationships do not occur by accident. Great organizations do not develop through osmosis. Great championship sports teams don't just happen. All great teams, at home, work, or play operate within a team environment and modality that provides for each member of the team identifying and sharing his or her ambitions. Then the team asks honest questions of itself. The team asks questions to determine if there are common goals and interests amongst all teammates. The team asks questions to assess if there is a commitment to achieving something great. The owner of a professional sports team with an ambition of erecting a great championship franchise requires players committed to and ambitious about winning championships, not players simply obsessed with an idea of getting rich. Company CEO's, presidents, administrators and owners with ambitions of building great organizations and companies require employees at all levels that are armed with commitment and ambitions congenial to the overall vision of the organization; not employees simply motivated by the pay check at the end of the week or the bonuses at the end of the year. Enron was an example of such a company with too many employees motivated by weekly pay checks and annual bonuses. A man or woman who yearns for a great marital relationship requires a partner that is committed and also ambitious about having a great marital relationship, not a partner simply in the relationship for self-serving reasons as sex, finances, or security. In any of your situations, either at home, work or play, you have to ask questions to ascertain if you are truly engaged in a situation that will provide you the environment in which great accomplishments will be achieved. You have to have those tough conversations about the ambitions of everyone involved. You have to understand if the ambitions of your teammates are aligned for success or aligned for failure.

Develop creature habits today that will ensure you will always have the ability to identify the alignment of your ambitions with the ambitions of those on your team. If your ambitions and the ambitions of your teammate or mates do not align, have the courage to have open dialogue and determine if proper alignment can be achieved. And if you determine proper alignment is not possible or not worth the effort, as it is in some cases, play yourself "BIG" (Brilliant – Intelligent – Great) and find another team to play on that supports your ambitions to achieve greatness. Listen to John D. Rockefeller and don't hang around simply for the money. Give up the good and go be as great as you want to be. Always, always, always play yourself "BIG!" Identify your ambitions so you can always play yourself "BIG" at home, work, or play.

THE SECOND CHALLENGE:

FIRST EXERCISE

1. What makes you so brilliant?

2. Why are you so intelligent?

3. What makes you so great?

4. Why do you play yourself small when you are so "BIG?"

5. Who in your life belittles your ambitions?

Now review the list of answers to the first 10 items in the first challenge and complete the following:

SECOND EXERCISE

1. Identify your ambitions and write them down in a separate section of your notebook or in a separate file on your computer.

2. Identify the ambitions of every member of all of your current teams.

a. Team 1: Current Personal Relationship

b. Team 2: Current Professional Relationship (*This team financially compensates you for your efforts*)

c. Team 3: Current Extra-curricular Relationship (*This team is outside of your personal and professional relationship teams*)

3. Identify 10 reasons why you believe your current team(s) provides an environment that supports your ambitions to achieve greatness.

4. List three reasons why you should leave your current team(s).

a. Team 1: Current Personal Relationship

b. Team 2: Current Professional Relationship

c. Team 3: Current Extra-curricular Relationship

5. Identify 10 reasons why you believe your current team(s) does not provide an environment that supports your ambitions to achieve greatness.

a. Team 1: Current Personal Relationship

b. Team 2: Current Professional Relationship

c. Team 3: Current Extra-curricular Relationship

6. List three reasons why you should remain with your current team(s).

a. Team 1: Current Personal Relationship

b. Team 2: Current Professional Relationship

c. Team 3: Current Extra-curricular Relationship

Self-discovery is such an integral element to identifying your ambitions. The above exercises are practically impossible to complete if you have no self-awareness or self-understanding. Self-discovery helps you to first say what you want to be great at. Your true talents, brilliance, intelligence, and capabilities are barometers for what you have the God given volition and ability to do. Self-discovery assists you in identifying your ambition.

Ambition gives you the courage to say you can when others tell you that you can not. Ambition tells you that whatever the endeavor requires, you will meet the challenge. With courage and confidence at your sides, tell yourself just how great you want to become, and then do whatever it takes. Realize that becoming great may entail waving good-bye to your current associations (home, work, or play) and taking your "BIG" self elsewhere.

When I realized my ambitions to become a professional business consultant and performance coach, I also realized my place of employment did not provide the proper environment or modality for me becoming a great business consultant or great performance coach. I knew in my heart I would have to one day say good-bye to this team and commission another winning team if I was to seriously pursue my desire to become what I so strongly wanted. My talent aligned perfectly with my passion for becoming a Peak Performance consultant. My life experiences, education, and employment history had delivered me to this apex where my talents, ambition and vision aligned properly for a career in helping others manage their personal and professional lives. My talents, ambition and vision were not properly aligned for high achievement and great success at this particular place of employment. This misaligned ambition and vision was the root cause of my disgruntlement with my job situation. I simply was not happy with my job. So I made a decision that it was finally time to do what I have always wanted to do. I knew I had to take my "BIG" self elsewhere and do whatever was required of me to become the person I wanted to be. My decision to become as great as I wanted to be is what caused me to sit down with a focused purpose and write this book that you now read. I am living proof that when you identify your ambitions and have the courage and confidence to follow your dreams, BIG things will happen in life.

"First say what you would be; and then do what you have to."

—Epictetus

You may find yourself in similar situations at home, work or play where you are experiencing feelings or thoughts of the big D's of dissatisfaction within your team environment(s); Disengagement, Disinterest, Disdain, and/or Discord, now or in the future. If so, be willing to accept the fact that any combination of the big D's of dissatisfaction in your team environment will severely cripple your ability to be successful and happy on the team. Don't blame your teammates for being who they are. Simply understand that there are no common identifiable ambitions to produce a common purpose to drive the team to success, happiness, and greatness. The very reason for identifying your ambitions and the ambitions of your teammates is so you can make this very determination. Take this task very seriously. Becoming as great as you want to be is paramount to you having the unwavering fortitude to act on your own behalf to preserve your right to manifest your true will. You are playing yourself small when you make a decision to intentionally remain in situations characterized by your feelings or thoughts of disengagement, disinterest, disdain, and/or discord. You also place your team at a grave disadvantage when you harbor and allow yourself to be influenced by such counterproductive devices. No team can be successful when members integral to its vibrant existence are disengaged from the overall vision, disinterested in any common cause, and void of any passion or true purpose for success. Essentially, no one benefits when there is a dearth of ambition, excitement, fervency, and meaning amongst key players in the organization, on the team, or in the relationship.

Third Exercise

1. Pause here and seriously contemplate your curent situations on your current teams. Review your answers to the questions you provided on item numbers 4 and 6 above in the second exercise.

2. Now consider both exercises above in their entirety. Determine if any serious and firm feelings or thoughts of disengagement, disinterest, disdain, and/or discord are due to contrasting ambitions between you and your teammate(s). If so, develop a plan to address each issue.

3. Determine, unequivocally, if each of your current teams have ambitions, purposes, goals, and interests that align with your ambitions.

4. Based on these determinations, make a decision for your life that is influenced by your ambitions. And whatever you decide, always play yourself "BIG."

"Ambition can be an insatiable and implacable passion. Understand that ambition alone will never guarantee success. All the ambition in the world will not help you catch a fish if there are no fish in the water."

—Ronald T. Hickey

After determining that your ambitions align with your teammate(s) or after making the decision to move to another team where ambition alignment is possible, make sure you have positioned yourself for success. Your ambitions must be coupled to attainable goals. Your ambitions and the ambitions of your organization will be in vain, no matter the level of or the commitment to ambition, if your situation provides for no possibility of success. If you are ambitious about traveling to the moon, understand that your ambition alone will not propel you to outer space; you will need great ambition and a damn good space rocket. If you know your ambitious endeavors will require a team of individuals to be successful then don't go at it alone. Great marriages require two great individuals and a great support system. So many women go into a marriage with an expectation of having a great marital relationship with a great guy; but they knowingly marry a person who is a womanizer, shifty, and none-productive. This act conveys low ambition.

Great companies require great people at all rungs of the organizational ladder; but companies, time and time again, hire people who are not qualified for the job they are hired to perform. I find it so hard to believe that companies continue to hire a person after only interviewing the person just once and for only a few minutes. How can one possibly assess ambition, talent, and vision utilizing such an empty process? The American work environment is quickly deteriorating because so many people are misaligned with the tasks they are hired to perform. Unfortunately, people are misaligned because the hiring process is defunct in most organizations and human resource personnel increasingly lack the qualifications to make proper staffing decisions.

We make similar decisions in our personal lives as well. I know several individuals who decided to marry after having known the other person only a few months. That process speaks volumes about the two individuals involved and their commitment to having a great relationship. Many years are typically required before the universe reveals to a person his or her true purpose, vision, and ambitions in life. The universe allows us to mature our minds and develop our talents. We make many changes in life along the way. And when we are ready to accept our true purpose, that lifelong pursuit that will make us happy beyond our wildest dreams; the transformative power of our ambitions and passions move us into complete alignment with the very things necessary for the successful journey to greatness. This alignment is a time consuming process that can not be circumvented. Circumvention of universal laws leads to destitution and despair. Look at every individual who married the wrong person at the wrong time. Look at every organization with mediocre employees at every level hired too quickly just because some human resource specialist is driven by the rate at which he or she can close-out the job requisitions in his or her files. Almost every job I have ever held has required me to work with individuals who were not even remotely qualified to do the jobs they were hired to perform. This identifies a failure of the human resource function that needs to improve in every organization.

When you apply for a job with an organization and are fortunate enough to be invited to interview for a position, pay close attention to the process. Realize that the process you are subjected to will be the similar process utilized for selecting everyone you will be required to work with. Learn to desire and appreciate a rigorous hiring process that is truly modeled for finding and selecting the best person for the position. If you feel the process was sufficient for determining your talent, ambition, and vision; then there can be an expectation for ambition alignment within the organization. I have actually rejected employment offers made to me when I was selected after having interviewed only once for a 30 minute time period. I have learned from experience that those organizations will result in job dissatisfaction for me. I am at a point in my life where I have been very successful and need more than just a pay check. My ambitions are much more aloft than simply getting rich. If you are the hiring manager, don't feel obligated to continue to fail your organization simply because the human resource function is inadequate. Develop fair and legal processes for determining if the people coming into your company have the talent, ambition and long-term vision that are in complete alignment with the overall vision and needs of your team. Your ability to achieve greatness depends on it. Without these processes, we potentially find ourselves fishing with the ambition of becoming a great angler in waters where there are no fish.

"The man who understands how something is done will always be employed. The man who understands why something is done, will always be the boss of the man who only knows how. But the woman who bends the arc of sexism and owns the company understands the true and ultimate power of ambition."

—Ronald T. Hickey

A woman once wrote, "*A woman who aspires to be equal with men, lacks ambition.*" Identifying your ambitions and the ambitions of others is essential to your well being. Equally essential to the ultimate manifestation of your greatness is the understanding of the true and quintessential power of ambition. Remember, ambition raises us above ourselves; above our failures, above our obstacles, and above our limits. Ambition is the driving force that pushes us forward when everything in our lives tells us we can not succeed. Ambition is the life form that creates an unyielding desire in a man to become President of the United States of America, despite the fact that he was raised by a single white mother after his black father abandoned him and his mom when he was only 2 years old. Ambition orders the steps of a little girl born and raised in an impoverish trailer park and takes her to the stage of a theatre where she accepts the Academy award for Best Actress. Ambition has no limits. It will deliver you to any destination you so choose. Do you want to be a great husband in a great marriage? If so, identify your ambition. Do you want to promote to the CEO of your company? Then identify the ambition to do so and properly align that ambition with others with the ambition to take you there. Do you want to become as great as you want to be? All you need to do is understand the true power of ambition; and if you doubt its true power in the slightest you may want to consider what it has allowed Bill Gates, Oprah Winfrey, Will Smith, Jack Welch, Tiger Woods, Barack Obama, Hillary Swank, Jamie Foxx, Steve Jobs, Joel Osteen, T.D. Jakes, Larry King, Jay Leno, Steven King, J.K. Rowling, Lance Armstrong, Venus Williams, Serena Williams, and so many others to accomplish in their lives. Ambition has the power to do the same for you. Identify your ambitions and the ambitions of others. Your greatness depends on you doing so!

You have made a determination to follow your ambitions. I believe that is the very reason you are reading this book. Your purpose has become the deepest meaning in your life. The walls of your mind reverberates the sound of your joy. This is the moment of your new beginning. Look around you; all auspicious evidence conveys that the universe is positioned for your orderly progression to success. Resist the temptation to move hastily and take time to enjoy this moment in front of you. Enjoy the resolve of your mind, the boldness of your first steps, the innocence of your expectations, the sanguinity of your hope, and the faith of your heart. You will never feel this way again. Now start by making a decision to commit to your ambitions you have identified. Nothing outside and beyond these ambitions should matter to you at this point. In this condition of solitude and vulnerability you must navigate the challenges of your life's pursuit down the pathway to greatness. You alone must vow to make something of this life God has given you. No one can do it for you. There is a transformative effect to this knowledge that provides you with the necessary incitement for engaging life on this highest plateau of spiritual atonement. With this one devotion to a lifetime of commitment, the universe has set in route to your location everything you require for the journey. The favorable signs that are now so vivid to you bear witness to this response of the universe. Your unwavering commitment to your ambitions will give birth to your success. Congratulations! You have taken the second step toward becoming as great as you want to be.

Challenge Three

Properly Align and Manage Your Talents for Success

"If you have talent, use it in every which way possible. Don't hoard it. Don't dole it out like a miser. Spend it lavishly like a millionaire intent on going broke."

—Brendan Francis

A good friend of mine came to me years ago and asked for my opinion. He and his wife, at that time, were in constant conflict concerning which one of them should have the lead roll in managing their family finances. My friend asked if he should manage the finances because he was the better financial person between he and his wife; even though he would rather not, or should he allow is wife to manage the family finances because she was more passionate about doing the job; even though she was not the best person for the job. My friend stated that his wife routinely paid the bills late and was not disciplined enough to stick to an agreed upon budget. He said when he is in control, the bills are never paid late, they are always within budget, and there is extra money for savings each month. I asked my friend what his intentions were in attempting to come to an equitable solution to balancing the emotional needs of his wife with the overall and paramount need for his family to be financially healthy. I asked if his intentions were to build a winning family structure that was flexible enough to adapt seamlessly to a variety of different financial situations or to build harmony in his marriage by keeping his wife happy by yielding to her psychological need to fill an emotional void in her life by acting as the family Chief Financial Officer. Unfortunately, emotional harmony and winning environments are often competing atmospheres in many marriages. I suggested to my friend that he handle the finances if his goal was to build a winning team, and I also stated that his wife should be allowed to handle the finances if making her happy was more important than winning. I told him that the team would suffer and to prepare for some defeats if he was not prepared to properly align his talents and his wife's talents with family tasks, especially those as important as managing the money. Money problems tend to be a popular reason many relationships ultimately experiences a demise.

In a team setting, the player with the greatest talent for a particular position should always be given first preference for playing at that particular position, if the team intends to give itself the greatest opportunity for success. I recall playing sports in middle and high school back in Tennessee. For those who may not be aware, local sports at the middle and high school levels in many communities in many of the Southern states of the United States are bigger than sports on the college and professional level; and winning becomes everything. With that being the case, many of the kids at the middle and high schools I attended had wealthy parents that would use their financial power to ensure their child had the opportunity to play sports in the position the child or parent most desired; irrespective of the child's athletic ability and/or natural talent at the particular position. As a result, athletic abilities and natural talents were more often, than not, misaligned and mismanaged on the teams I played on.

One year our baseball team made it to the state tournament. Prior to one game, and just before game time, I overheard the head coach and the assistant coach discussing who should start at the shortstop position. The choice was between a kid that was the best at the position on our team and a kid with mediocre skills, but with a wealthy father. The head coach stated he did not want to loose the support of the wealthy parent. The assistant coach asked the head coach if he intended to win the game or make a parent happy? The rich kid started, and we lost the game. The rich kid made two critical errors on defense and provided no offense for our team during the game. When asked by the assistant coach as to why the rich kid was not replaced after his second error, the head coach replied, "Benching him would destroy his confidence in himself." The assistant coach asked, "What about the other kids on the team? What about their needs and hard work?"

Just as my high school baseball coach decided against a winning line-up, my friend with the finanical dilemma chose harmony in his marriage. The financial conflicts that were generated as a result of that decision gave birth to many other marital problems for my friend and his ex-wife. The marriage eventually ended in a nasty divorce. The misaligned and mismanaged financial talents in his marriage prevented the marriage from having any possibility for success. Likewise, just like my friend and his ex-wife and my high school baseball team, many individuals, relationships, teams, associations, and organizations are not positioned for peak performance and optimum success because talent is misaligned and mismanaged. Organizations, teams, families and other groups of people are not prepared for success because individuals are in positions they are not qualified for. We make these decisions based on a number of factors that are often times geared only to benefit a few individuals and not the whole body of people. I know many of us have been in or are in situations where we know talent is misaligned. People get promotions based on personal relationships instead of professional decisions intended to best benefit the organization. If your goal is to win and succeed, ensure you properly align your talents and the talents of your teammates. Manage for success. Fill every position, whether at home or at work, with the best talent you have at your disposal, and utilize those talents like a millionaire intent on going broke; using the words of Brendan Francis again. If you don't, you should not have any false expectations of being successful in your endeavors.

"Everyone according to their talent, and every talent according to its work."

—French Proverb

I believe one of the greatest calamities of life is to die with talent unused. Each of us has the talent to be great at something. When we are able to match our talents with our work, success becomes us. When Ray Kroc matched his talent with his work at a very mature age, success became the McDonald's fast food empire. Ray Kroc was born in 1902 and tried his hand at being a salesman, a jazz musician, and a band member before he purchased the fast-food restaurant, McDonald's, from Dick and Mac McDonald in 1961. He amassed a wealth of over $500 million during his time. Ray Kroc's story epitomizes what your life can become when your talent is matched with your work. When Johnny Carson matched his talent with his work, success became the best in late night television talk shows for 30 years. Johnny Carson began his adult life by serving in the United States Navy and worked for several radio stations before his unlikely chance to do television. He would eventually amass monetary and real estate property wealth in the neighborhood of $300 million. Johnny Carson was an example of professional talent and natural ability that was properly aligned and managed for success. When J.K. Rowling matched her talent with her work, success became the most successful child fantasy book series, Harry Potter. Miss Rowling worked as a teacher earlier in her life. She envisioned the Harry Potter story during a train ride in 1990, several years before she was successful in publishing her first book. Before becoming a published author, J.K. Rowling gave birth to her only child and divorced in the same year of 1993. After her divorce, she lived on welfare and wrote her first Harry Potter book in cafes. The first twelve publishers she submitted her book to turned the book down. The Harry Potter series, to date, has sold over 400 million copies. J.K. Rowling was reported to be worth approximately $800 million in 2008. In approximately a ten year span, J.K. Rowling went from being a single mother on welfare to essentially a billionaire. J.K. Rowling represents the ultimate in properly aligning and managing your talents for success. Live according to your talents, and let your talents be according to your work. If you do so, you could very well reach success parallel to Ray Kroc, Johnny Carson, or J.K. Rowling.

Talent has to be properly managed for you to be successful. It is not enough to simply possess the ability to do something. You have to exercise that ability before anything can be produced. Once you start to produce something, this is the very point in which proper management becomes critical for success to be achieved; for any production must be managed to ensure goals are met and intentions come to complete fruition. Using J.K. Rowling again as an example, what if she never exercised her imagination and writing ability? Fortunately for all of us, she did. Once her talent began to produce the Harry Potter character, Miss Rowling had to manage her productions. Her proper management of her abilities and what it produced is precisely what allowed her to remain true to her calling, despite being turned down by the first twelve publishers she submitted her book to. She very easily could have become disenfranchised by the process and given up on her dream. Miss Rowling stayed in her lane and managed her life and her dream in a manner that resulted in her success. Writing in cafes were part of her management plan. Do you have a management plan for what your life is producing? Do you have an understanding of what it takes to be successful in your chosen profession?

You must have a complete understanding of what is required of a profession before you can develop a management plan for being successful in the profession. For some professions, matriculating a course of study in college wanes in comparison to studying for and passing the exam that allows a person to practice that profession for a living. I know several attorneys who have had to take their state BAR exam multiple times before they passed the exam. I know some who have taken the exam 10 or more times and have not passed the exam yet. Passing the exam determines if a person has the ability to practice the profession. Studying for the exam must be properly managed for success to be achieved. The exam separates those who have the ability to practice law from those who only have the ability to study and pass college courses. Passing the college courses simply gives one the opportunity to begin production on an endeavor that must be greatly managed before a person can ever legally practice law. Once a person passes the BAR exam, he or she must continue to manage his or her abilities and talents to ultimately become a successful attorney. Those who manage their law careers the best become known as the F. Lee Bailey's and Johnnie Cochran's of their career field. The very fortunate few are known as United States Supreme Court Justices. A Supreme Court Justice is an ex-law student who managed his or her career extremely well. That management includes advanced levels of academics at the best law schools that provide for prestigious job offers, high levels of job performances, impressive and impeccable professional achievements and personal sacrifice, and well managed networks of movers and shakers. Success is not a product of happenstance; success is the result of an excellent plan for life management of the work your natural abilities produce.

Professional golfers often speaks of "course management" when they describe their ability to win golf tournaments. While some are recognized as the world's top golfers, their talents simply provide them with one of the best golf swings in the sport. These top golfers understand that they must go out and manage that talented golf swing on the golf course if they wish to be successful. As those of us who have ever swung a golf club at any level of play know so well, winning a golf tournament requires much more than simply having a good golf swing. You have to manage your game, manage the course, and manage your life to be a golf champion. Professional golfer John Daly's rise and fall in the sport attests to that fact. John Daly was one of those golfers who had one of the best golf swings in the sport. But much of his life and his game have suffered tremendously from his inability to properly manage his life and his golf game for success, on and off the golf course. You find this the case with many would be great athletes. Their natural talents and abilities produce a professional sports career, but their inability to properly manage their lives ruin the careers they work so hard to secure for themselves. Ability alone does not guarantee success or aide in maintaining success once you have achieved it. Ability must be well managed your entire life if you want to be successful your entire life.

Managing your happy marriage and other healthy personal relationships are examples of successes that will experience catastrophic failures if we allow ourselves to think we can just place them in auto-pilot and have them continue to be successful. Auto-pilot is not a viable management plan if you intend to have a healthy, happy and prosperous marriage. You can't just ignore your husband, wife, domestic partner, or the person you are romantically involved with and think things will remain "hunky-dory". All successes have to be well managed for the successes to be sustainable over significant time spans, particularly love relationships. Our personal relationships require the most management of any endeavor in which we engage for them to continue to be successful year after year after year. Having the ability to be a good husband or good wife means absolutely nothing if you don't put that talent to use to make your mate happy. Allowing your mate to perform tasks within the relationship when he or she is not talented enough to perform the tasks successfully is not being a good husband or wife if the poor performance ultimately gives rise to issues that causes irreconcilable differences.

Personal relationships are by far our toughest engagements in life. That is why we must give our absolute best in our personal relationships. We must exercise our best abilities at all times. The very moment we relax is the very moment problems develop and drive a wedge between us and our spouse. I don't want this to be a narrative on marriage counseling, I don't have anything to offer to that subject but my own experiences. My wife pays the bills and handles the finances in my house because she is the best at money matters. I handle tasks that I am the best at. Our marriage is no fairytale, but we don't allow talent misalignment and talent mismanagement to exaggerate the normal marital problems that can drive people apart and make everyone unhappy. A marriage is one team that should always have the best players at every position. I know thinking of a marriage relationship as a team can be a challenge for some. I know I struggled with the concept until my wife told me that I was using my talents and abilities to do a great job at work, but I was not giving the same effort at home. I want to win in my marriage. My wife and I and our children are now a team, and I expect us to be champions one day.

Managing your career can be similar to managing your personal relationships. Everyone involved in your success at work can be considered a teammate. Understanding that winning as a team determines the level of your success that will help you realize that each individual exists as a dependent event along your pathway to success. Their actions influence the quality of your existence. You being as successful as possible depends on everyone around you performing at a peak level. If anyone on your team is not talented enough, or if you are not talented enough, you must create and implement a talent realignment and talent management plan for your career. You may need to go back to school to get that promotion you desire. You may need to transfer to another department to gain access to the boardroom. Using a United States Supreme Court Justice as an example again, imagine the ongoing education throughout the career of a Supreme Court Justice. Imagine the number of times they had to change jobs, positions and career paths. Imagine how important it was for each of them to understand the talent and abilities of everyone around them. Their careers have always been dependent on those around them, on their team.

Understanding the abilities and talents of individuals on the team is vitally important to you having the ability to properly align talent for peak performance. If we are unequivocally aware of the depth of the talent pool, we can best deploy our resources for optimum achievement. This knowledge also allows us to identify weakness in the talent pool. In addition, proper management of talent (ensuring every individual is tasked and rewarded in a manner that supports their individual ambitions and the ambitions of the team) is the sure way to talent retention and recruitment, although talent recruitment begins and ends with the individual being recruited.

A few years ago I was working as a Production Manager in a Hi-Tech electronics manufacturing facility in Silicon Valley. I had invited and scheduled applicants to interview for a maintenance electrician position. One applicant had stated on his resume that he had experience working as an electrical systems troubleshooter while enlisted in the United States Navy. I invited this particular applicant to the interview process because I initially enlisted into the United States Navy as an electrician and knew first hand of the training and education provided by the Navy in this particular skilled craft discipline. Of course the applicant had no knowledge of my military background that placed me at a position of advantage with this particular applicant. I was able to ask him specific questions about the Navy's electrical training and education. After asking the applicant only three questions, it was very obvious to me that he had not been trained or educated as an electrician in the United States Navy. While this individual could regurgitate some basic language of the electrical trade; he was, by no stretch of the imagination, an experienced, trained and educated electrician. He knew he did not possess the necessary talent to perform the job of a maintenance electrician in an electronics manufacturing operation. He knew he did not have the ability to perform the functions of an electrician at a "High Worth" level of rating. This individual would not have been successful in this position, and the company would have been disadvantaged by his lack of talent for the job. Imagine if I was not advantaged with the knowledge I had. What could have been the outcome? What has been the outcome when the interview process failed the applicant and the organization? While organizations have a responsibility for developing a selection process that does not provide for unqualified individuals being offered employment, the primary responsibility is with the individual to not apply for positions in which natural and learned talents are not available for ensuring success.

"You have to have confidence in your ability, and then be tough enough to follow through."

—Rosalynn Carter

The responsibility for knowing who you are and what you are capable of must be embraced in every relationship in our lives. We must identify, recognize, and determine our own ability to be successful as someone's husband, wife, father, and/or mother before we communicate to someone that we are ready to marry or have children. Likewise, a person must know his or her ability before he or she accepts a position to run the anchor leg of a 4 X 100 meter relay. Don't say you have ability you know you do not have. You must have confidence in your ability, and your team should be able to have confidence in your ability, as well. Your success depends on your teammates' abilities, and their success depends on your abilities. In a team environment, we must understand how our actions affect the overall operation and consider our actions as critically important dependent events for the success of everyone involved. On a track team, each person must assess his or her own talent for sprinting, and whatever that level of sprinting ability, be tough enough to follow through.

I ran several sprint events on my high school track team. Now I knew I was never going to break any land speed records. I knew my limitations on the track. Plus, the track was one place that would truly reveal your speed, or lack thereof, at some point or another. The truth would eventually be known by all. One year a new kid had transferred to the school. He expressed interest in the track team. He informed our track coach that he had a very fast 100 yard sprint time; the race was not called the 100 meters back then. While he said he had quick feet, I noticed a lack of confidence in his demeanor. I knew kids who were as quick as lightning, and they were very boastful about their abilities. This new kid conveyed nothing that resembled such confidence. Nevertheless, as a result of the new kid's self-confessions, he was placed on the 4 X 100 yards relay team as the anchor.

I normally ran the anchor, but gladly moved to another position on the relay team because I knew I did not run the best anchor leg. I just happened to be the fastest on a relay team of mediocre sprinters. No one had ever seen this new kid sprint before, but we accepted our coach's position. The new kid was unable to practice the week leading up to his first race on our relay team. The coach accepted all of his excuses and was convinced that the new kid was as fast as he had advertised himself to be. Race day finally came, and there was much anticipation surrounding this supposedly new sprinter with self-confessed lightning speed. Well, as I mentioned earlier, the track will eventually reveal your talents for what they truly are. During the highly anticipated relay race, not only had the new kid failed to exhibit the kind of speed he spoke so highly of, he did not even have the stamina to sprint the entire 100 yards. Yes, he fell to the ground exhausted before crossing the finish line. Everyone on the team was humiliated and disgusted by his poor performance.

Convincing someone to give you the opportunity to do something that you know you are not capable of can often times prove to be an easy task because the person you are convincing really wants everything you say to be true. But when you are void of any remote talent for the position, you place yourself and your team in a position to inevitably fail. Everyone wanted this kid to be as fast, or faster, than he said he was. Don't put yourself and those who depend on you in a position to fail because you have over inflated yourself. Don't subject yourself and your team to the humiliation of not even being able to finish the race. If you can, say you can with confidence. If you can not, say you can not with conviction. You must be honest with yourself, your spouse, your employer, your teammates, and others who depend on you. Your honesty about your abilities is the first step to proper talent alignment in all of your relationships, at home, work or play. The first two challenges of this book provide you with the framework for being honest about the person you are, what you are capable of, and what you are ambitious about. The first two challenges encourage you to identify your strengths. Play to those strengths if success and happiness are your goals. Do not present yourself as a talented musician when, like me, you can not even read sheet music. Everyone is talented at something. Identify that something. Your success depends on it.

"We are always more anxious to be distinguished for a talent which we do not possess, than to be praised for the fifteen which we do possess."

—Mark Twain, Mark Twain's Autobiography

Once you have identified and fully understand your true talents, strive incessantly to properly align your talents for success. Properly align your talents for success in the right job with the right employer. Do not interview for employment positions you know you are not talented for because you may just get the job; and then you will be a miserable and stressed out employee because you will be in way over your head and your lack of talent will be unable to support you successfully. If you are currently in a situation at work where your skill set wanes in comparison to the experience, training, education and knowledge actually required to be highly successful in the position; commit to finding employment that is a better match and more suitable and in proper alignment with your abilities. Your very health may depend on you doing so. I have learned over the years that the majority of stressed out employees are so stressed out because they lack all of the necessary tools to effectively perform all the functions of their job. People tend to stay in such positions at the detriment of their health and their company. And companies can only properly manage talent that is properly aligned within the organization. You can not manage talent if there is no talent to be managed. Many companies and organizations have jumped on the new ban wagon of "Talent Management" as an operational approach to addressing staffing needs. I think it is excellent to consider properly managing the talent in your employee pool. The only problem is there are so many employees within an organization who are improperly aligned with the overall vision and needs of the organization, and to thin out such misaligned employees presents an enormous task for any organization. This massive amount of improperly aligned employees creates a formidable challenge to talent management as a tool; so formidable, in fact, many companies become too overwhelmed and discard all attempts at true talent management. An organization must have the right employees already onboard before the organization can effectively engage in successful talent management. As my grandfather use to say, "You can't squeeze blood from a turnip."

"Whatever you are by nature, keep to it; never desert your line of talent. Be what nature intended you for and you will succeed."

—Sydney Smith

Talent alignment involves the process of scientifically and methodically identifying the human traits, professional skill sets, educational backgrounds, and work experience profiles that an employee must possess to be highly skilled and successful in a particular role or specific task or classification within an organization. Talent management refers to the strategic process of identifying, attracting, capturing, developing, integrating, and retaining new highly skilled workers; and re-developing, re-deploying, retaining, and promoting current highly skilled workers in your company. These two integral processes require that human resource departments expand their current skills and talent beyond their current capacities. Harrah's Entertainment, Inc.; in the casino gaming industry, understood the need for this critical process in the late 1990's. When other casinos were moving to a business strategy of building "must see" gambling and entertainment properties, Harrah's focused on an operational strategy of aligning and managing their talent pool. While Harrah's business strategy was a marketing-based strategy, they understood that they would not get the marketing piece right if they failed to address the people factor within their organization. As a result, Harrah's developed a talent alignment and management process that asked the question, "Are we selecting the best person for the job, or just someone who can meet the minimum job requirements?" To assist in this endeavor, Harrah's developed two tests, a 20 questions test for entry-level employees and a longer (more than 20 questions) test for entry-level supervisors; in addition to the individual interview. For higher-level employees, Harrah's also utilized standardized testing instruments such as the Hogan Personality Inventory, Watson-Glaser Critical Thinking Appraisal, leadership opinion questionnaire, and the Gordon Personal Profile Inventory. Additionally, a director of assessment with a Ph.D. in Psychometrics was hired by Harrah's to assist in understanding the human psychological profile of all potential employees. Harrah's goal was to hire the "best person for the job." A company must be able to identify, attract, capture, develop, and retain great employees if the company wants to become great in it's industry.

"I do not want to die ... until I have faithfully made the most of my talent and cultivated the seed that was placed in me until the last small twig has grown."

—Käthe Kollwitz

Our personal relationships should be fashioned by a process in a manner that is similiar to the hiring process that Harrah's developed. In relationships, our goals should be to select the "best person for the job." Great people produce great relationships. Bad people produce bad relationships. As in the employment selection process, personal relationships should also include a socialization process focused on the human profile. Personal relationships, as with professional relationships, need to reconnect with the human element of the individuals involved and focus on understanding what people really need to excel in their human endeavors, whether at home or on the job.

Sure, all people need tools, proper environments, and training to be successful in supporting the business strategy or the prosperity of the family; but individuals also need to be socialized into the operational and family structure. This is precisely the area in which many American relationships and companies are failing miserably. Just as Harrah's understood in the late 1990's, if you don't get the people part right, you will not succeed.

Getting the people part right is so critical in this "knowledge-worker" age of employment in the 21st century. Companies have to systematically align and manage all employees in one of only two directions in the organizations; up or out. A standard must be established, published, and enforced that conveys to every employee at every level that there is a company culture of expectations that all employees develop and maintain a "high-worth" rating within the organization. The days of the "minimum standard" employee must be ushered out of your operational strategy if your organization's business strategy is going to remain competitive in this current business climate around the globe. Employees who fail to maintain a "high-worth" rating should be aggressively managed out of the organization. Remember, mediocre employees produce mediocre products that produce mediocre companies. One mediocre, or "minimum standard", employee will influence another employee to become mediocre. Before long, your company will have an unfavorable and significant growth of mediocre employees who will be working counter-productive to the company's goal of business success. And given enough time, your company will be just another mediocre company.

If your organization is in the unfortunate situation of a Union-Management atmosphere, look no farther; your significantly growing pool of mediocre employees is within the union. In America the evolvement of the union into what it represents today exists as the most prominent source of mediocrity within any organization. I understand that this statement may be somewhat controversial, but look at the data. The poorest functioning organizations in America are those operating in a Union-Management atmosphere. The union is self-serving to its members and not serving the bottom line of the organization. The protections provided by American union agreements with companies are the very vices that allow employees to elect mediocrity without consequence. Unions started out with a very valiant purpose in America; but they have evolved into what they represent today. American employment unions promote the "minimum requirement" concept and resist vigorously against the "high-worth" rating concept in employees.

To help establish the "high-worth" rating within your organization, develop a highly effective, comprehensive, and practical employee performance evaluation process. This process need not be as sophisticated as the process utilized by Harrah's Entertainment, Inc., but the process should involve comparing each employee to task performance standards from leading organizations in your industry. Which process is the best is not the scope of this book. There are many processes to choose from that should prove extremely beneficial to your company in this endeavor.

Utilizing an employee performance evaluation process, all employees in the organization should be divided into three groups; A, B, and C. Many of the employee evaluations that I have been subjected to at the various employers I worked for over the years had three basic categories: "Does Not Meet Expectations", "Meets Expectations", or "Exceeds Expectations." Most evaluators went for the "Meets Expectations" rating. This provided for the least amount of work on their part because it required no explanation. The evaluator was also required to justify a rating of either "Exceeds Expectations" or "Does Not Meet Expectations." The evaluator levitating toward "Meets Expectations" to lessen his or her own workload establishes intrinsic flaws in the evaluation process. Review the current employee performance evaluations in your organization. If you have a high percentage of employees rated at "Meets Expectations", your organization is mediocre at best. Mediocrity defines your organization because your employees are programmed to strive for a "Minimum Standard" performance rating, and not a "high-worth" performance rating.

The following is an explanation of an evaluation system that utilizes the A, B, and C group rating system:

"A" GROUP: This group of employees represents your "high-worth" rated employees. This group drives your bottom line. This group will normally be comprised of approximately 20% of your workforce and is responsible for approximately 70% of your organization's production. "High-worth" employees are the star performers. They are extremely talented and are self-actualized. "High-worth" employees are normally well aligned with the organization's overall vision. This does not mean their talent will always be well managed.

"B" GROUP: This group of employees represents your "minimum-standard" rated employees. This group supports your bottom line with minimum efforts. They do not go above and beyond. This group is normally controlled by policies and procedures. The "B" group normally makes up approximately 60% of your workforce and is responsible for approximately 25% of your organization's production. "Minimum-standard" employees are mediocre performers. They may have some hidden or undiscovered talent and are not self-actualized. Employees that simply meet expectations lack ambitions beyond the paycheck and have no interest in the organization's overall vision. This group of employees is normally highly mismanaged and misaligned within the organization.

"C" GROUP: This group of employees represents your "Fails To Meet Minimum Standard" rated employees. This group works against your bottom line with maximum effort. They work very hard at ensuring they do nothing for your organization. Group "C" normally represents approximately 20% of your workforce and is responsible for approximately 5% of your organization's production. "C" group employees cost an organization more to maintain than they actually produce. Most of your supervision man-hours are spent managing the poor performance of this group. "C" group employees should be managed out of your organization in an expedient manner. Some actually have the talent for great job performance, most do not; but everyone in this group severely lacks the ambition and vision necessary to ever be of benefit to your organization. Some in this group can be salvaged, but the cost may out weigh the benefits.

"Use your talents, for that is why they were made. What's a sun-dial in the shade?"

—Benjamin Franklin

THE THIRD CHALLENGE:

1. In your personal relationships, determine if each peson is the best person for accomplishing the tasks each person is responsible for.

2. Re-evaluate each of the relationships that you think involves talent misalignment, and align each person for success.

3. In your professional relationships, determine if each peson is the best person for accomplishing the tasks each person is responsible for.

4. Re-evaluate your teams if you think you or a teammate is misaligned for success.

5. Divide all of your teammates into the A, B, and C groups describe above.

6. Divide all the employees supervised by you into the A, B, and C groups.

7. Select the group you are in.

8. Select the group in which your teammates would place you.

9. Select the group in which your supervisor would place you.

10. If you determine you lack the necessary talent to be successful in any of your endeavors, develop your talents for success in your current situation or realign your talent in another endeavor where you can be successful.

11. Determine if the people around you are talented enough and if their talents are aligned so that you can be successful with this group. If not, determine if you can re-align and properly manage the available talent. If you can not, change teams.

12. Match your talents to your work. Do what nature intended for you to do. Remember, "What's a sun-dial in the shade?"

CHALLENGE FOUR

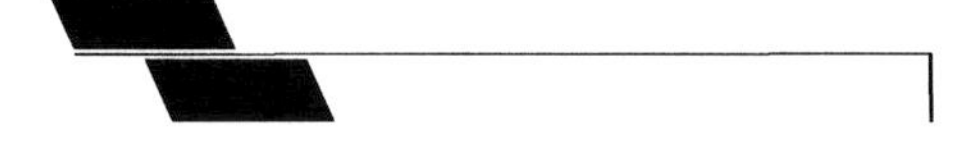

CREATE A FRAMEWORK FOR CRITICAL THINKING

"Most men would rather die, than think. Many do."

—Bertrand Russell

Critical thinking produces new perceptions, ideas and resolve. Resolve is the result of critically thinking through your problems, issues, situations, and conditions. Resolve is self-liberating. Our perceptions define our vision and desire for something. Our perceptions generate our thoughts, feelings and ideas. Ideas motivate us to action. With our own perceptions and fresh ideas, we step in the direction of personal success and unprecedented professional achievement. Furthermore, and perhaps most importantly, a solid framework for critical thinking eliminates the dependency on others to solve our every problem. Every individual should have the thinking ability to bring resolve to his or her issues. Such thinking ability should be unique and should come with ease.

So many individuals spend an enormous amount of time attempting to think like or be like someone else. No amount of thought will make you someone else. No amount of thought will make your organization just like some other organization. For this reason, everyone needs to understand that your thoughts must be consistent with your available talent, skills, and abilities if your thoughts are to be productive in delivering success to your human experience.

I had a childhood friend that was born with one normally functioning arm and with one physically deformed arm. The deformed arm was only about a third the size of his normal arm. It was much shorter and much thinner. The deformed arm lacked the normal muscular tissue of a normal arm. Aaron, my childhood friend, only had four fingers attached to his deformed arm and the fingers had physical impediments. They simply did not work like normal fingers. The bones in his deformed arm were so weak and fragile that he was required to wear a bone brace for protection. Aaron was extremely athletic like most young boys in my neighborhood. Anytime there was a pick-up game of basketball, baseball, football, or volleyball going on in the neighborhood, you could bet your last dollar he would be the first one ready to participate. Obviously his deformed arm presented him with a few challenges and disadvantages when participating in such sporting events. While I am sure he must have thought often of how his life would be different with two normal arms, I never heard him complain about his physical impediments. He did not dream and think of going to college on an athletic scholarship like many of us did. He understood his physical limitations. So Aaron did not waste time thinking like a kid who had two perfectly good arms. He knew that no amount of thought, however positive and focused, would produce a perfectly good arm where he had a deformed one. In college, Aaron took up a sport that none of the young boys in my neighborhood had ever been exposed to. He took up the sport of racquetball. This sport presented a situation where his deformed arm was no longer an impediment to his athletic excellence. I remember visiting my friend on the campus of the University of Tennessee, Chattanooga one weekend when I was home from college. In Aaron's sophomore year of 1983 at UTC, the most popular athlete on campus was a star basketball player named Gerald Wilkins. Gerald Wilkins was the brother of the more famous Dominique Wilkins and eventually would play a number of years in the NBA, just like is brother. The second most popular athlete on the campus of UTC was Aaron Hardgrove, the "one good armed-one bad armed" guy that absolutely no one on campus could beat in a racquetball match. The lesson I learned from Aaron Hargrove, now my adult friend, is that your thoughts and dreams have to be consistent with your available talents for you to be successful in life. Aaron did not have thoughts of going to the NBA like Gerald Wilkins did, even though both of them were very popular athletes on campus and both were very passionate about playing the sport of basketball. Aaron understood that his physical impediments prevented such an accomplishment. Aaron focused his thoughts on achievements that he knew he could attain.

God has blessed each of us with the ability to succeed once we develop the transformative mindset of understanding what we can and can not do as we focus our thoughts for success and happiness. Our thoughts must be consistent with and compliment our talents. What thoughts are you thinking that are not consistent with what you have the talent to bring into complete existence? Critical thinking will help you understand the concept that thinking alone does not cause success. Critical thinking will help you formulate a process for success that is absolutely unique to your unique situation, condition, and talent. In your thoughts, you have to play yourself. Critical thinking does not involve role playing. You must stay true to You! As Russell Simmons, the hip-hop mogul, states in his book, *Do You!, 12 Laws to Access the Power in You to Achieve Happiness and Success, "I always try to follow the Law of Do You, which stresses staying true to who you are and what you like in-*

stead of following trends." That's what Aaron Hardgrove did. He did himself.

It takes courage to grow up and turn out to be who you really are.

—E.E. Cummins

Through the 1990's and for the early part of the 21st century, while under the leadership of Jack Welch, the General Electric Company became the organization that many private sector, for profit, companies envied, attempted to mimic, and/or studied. Every CEO in America and many of them around the globe questioned what was it that Jack Welch and General Electric were doing that made them so great. So many companies wanted to clone themselves after General Electric; and many CEO's wanted to clone themselves after Jack Welch. What every company and every CEO that embarked upon this journey learned was every organization and every person is unique in their own existence. No two people are the same and no two organizations are the same. Organizations, like humans, must have the courage to grow up and turn out to be what and who they really are. To this day, no other company has become another General Electric and no other CEO has become another Jack Welch. General Electric became a great company because of the critical thinking of a unique team of professionals lead by Jack Welch. General Electric did not set out to clone itself after the image of another company. General Electric simply assessed the available talent in the company, the ambition of its workforce, and the vision of the organization, and had the courage to become who and what they were. Once the company understood exactly who it was, the company was able to determine what needed to change for the company to become a great company. Jack Welch recruited the necessary talent. He harvested that required ambition and provided the vision for greatness. When Jack Welch determined that a person's natural or acquired talent was insufficient, self-motivating ambition was absent, and individual vision was inconsistent with the vision of

General Electric; he made changes. And the changes were calculated, conscientious, and deliberate to support his vision for a great General Electric. Jack Welch was courageous.

In his book, Hope on a Tightrope, Dr. Cornel West writes, *"The road of inquiry is open to all travelers to the degree to which they are willing to allow their relative ignorance or naked power to be put in the spotlight."* To do such, requires a great degree of courage. Critical thinking is a courageous act of exposing your ignorance and weakness to gain wisdom and power. More often than not, the only witness to the truly courageous act of critical thinking is You. Ironically enough, coming to terms with one's ignorance and weakness requires the greatest amount of courage. In many ways it requires a person to die while living. Old beliefs and values die off so that new beliefs and values can birth, develop, and mature. Martin Luther King, Jr., one of the greatest critical thinkers of our times, Socratic in so many ways, once said, *"I am not willing to simply live and die for a mundane ideal or simply to further that ideology. I am willing to learn to die while I am alive, so I can live life more intensely and abundantly."* Henry David Thoreau, one of the greatest critical thinkers of all times, once said, *"I went up into the woods so that I could live life more deliberately, so that at life's end I would not look back and say I had not lived."* Both of these great figures of American history displayed enormous courage to think critically and bring resolve to the most important social issues during their time. Both were willing to allow their ignorance and weakness to die off so that their wisdom and power could birth, develop, and mature. By no stretch of the imagination am I suggesting that everyone aspire to such lofty levels of thought produced by Martin Luther King, Jr. or Henry David Thoreau. I am suggesting that if everyone is willing to elevate their mind, free their soul, and think their own thoughts, while allowing their ignorance and weakness to die off daily, life can be lived more intensely and much more abundantly. You, your teams, and all of your associations will be increased as a result of your willingness to act with such courage and commitment.

During the same time that General Electric was experiencing so much success, other companies, instead of deploying critical thinking to their own unique existence and lifting themselves up, were asking, "I wonder what GE would do in our situation?" Well, GE was never in the same situation as any other company. This is a good axample of what Bertrand Russell was referring to when he said (paraphrased), "*Many men and women would rather die than to think critically. Many of them do.*" A person or persons could verbalize such a question as, "What would GE do?", to provide for some very open and valuable dialogue amongst individuals attempting to generate some thoughts on a particular problem. Attempting to understand the viewpoints, opinions, positions, and wisdom of others can be a vitally important process of critical thinking; but it can not be mistaken for the end of critical thinking. You will not become the best possible You if your sole attempt at betterment only involves efforts of cloning yourself or your team in the image of another person or team. Critical thinking is the reason professional sports teams win Super Bowls, NBA Championships, and World Series. Sports teams study their opponents to conquer them, not to mimic them. Critical thinking put the first man on the moon and the last shuttle into orbit. President John F. Kennedy did not lead the United States in succeeding all nations in space exploration by means of thinking like any other Head of State. Critical thinking is the antidote to the poison that has killed many of our one-time successful companies. The New York Yankees organization has not won some 26 World Series Championships thinking like some other Major League Baseball organization. The United States of America did not win the race to the moon by thinking like Russia or China. Critical thinking is not the answer, but it is the process that provides the answer. Critical thinking lifts up your thoughts. And when you lift up your thoughts, you rise above your limits and failures. You conquer all your challenges and achieve the ultimate. The ultimate is growing to be You at your very best. Life is not about being another GE or Jack Welch. Life is about becoming the best You and making your organization the best it possibly can be. You can not view the world through someone else's eyes. Likewise, you can not lift yourself up recycling someone else's thoughts. You have to lift up your own thoughts, and lift them high to succeed high.

Now, just for a moment, let's consider critical thinking as an academic subject matter. **A DEFINITION OF CRITICAL THINKING:** Critical thinking is the intellectually guided discipline of actively and skillfully processing information gathered from or generated by a personal experience of some sort as a guide to belief and action. In its quintessential form, critical thinking is based on universal and intellectual values that transcend subject matter division in or of clarity, accuracy, precision, consistency, relevancy, sound evidence, good reasons, depth, breadth, complexity, simplicity, and fairness.

AN UNDERSTANDING OF CRITICAL THINKING:

Critical thinking can be seen as having two components: 1) a paradigm of information and belief generating and processing thoughts or skills, and 2) the habit, based on intellectual knowledge and commitment, of using those thoughts and/or skills to guide behavior. It is thus to be contrasted with: 1) the mere acquisition and retention of information alone, because it involves a particular way in which information is sought, gathered and treated; 2) the mere possession of a set of thoughts or skills, because it involves the continual use of them; and 3) the mere use of those skills, "as an exercise," without acceptance of their results.

Critical thinking varies according to the motivation underlying and provoking it. When grounded in selfish motives, it is often manifested in the skillful manipulation of ideas in service of one's own self-vested interest. As such, it is typically flawed in all of its modalities; however pragmatically successful it might prove to be. When given birth by the co-joining of fairness to intellectual integrity and passion to the proper modality of thinking, it is typically of a higher order intellectually and universally.

Critical thinking of any kind is never universal in any individual because everyone is subject to episodes of undisciplined or irrational thought. Its quality is therefore typically a matter of degree and dependent on, among other things, the quality and depth of experience in a given domain of thinking or with respect to a particular class of purposes, problems, questions, issues, situations, conditions, and/or considerations. No one is a critical thinker through-and-through, but only to such-and-such a degree; with so-and-so insights and routine misguidance, subject to varying degrees of tendencies toward self-delusion. For this reason, the development of critical thinking skills and dispositions should be a life-long endeavor.

A CONCEPT OF CRITICAL THINKING:

Critical thinking is self-motivated, self-guided, self-disciplined, and self-generated thought which acts to reason at the highest level of mental quality and human faculty. People who think critically consistently strive to live reasonably rational, empathic, and intellectual lives. They tend to be innately aware of the inherently and universally flawed nature of human thinking when left unexamined. Some critical thinkers strive to diminish themselves and think more universal. Some simply succumb to the power of egocentric and socio-centric tendencies. They use the intellectual tools that critical thinking offers by way of concepts and principles that enable them to conceptualize, generate, analyze, assess, and advance thinking ability. Critical thinkers work fervently to develop the intellectual virtues of intellectual integrity, intellectual humility, intellectual civility, intellectual empathy, intellectual sense of justice and confidence in reason. They realize that no matter how skilled they are as thinkers, they can always improve their reasoning abilities, and they will at times fall short of sound reasoning and become victims of irrationality, prejudices, biases, distortions, ill-gotten rules and traditions, taboos, folklore, self-interest, and vested interest germane to the human realm of existence. A critical thinker will strive to improve his or her life and the world in whatever possible manner and contributes to a more rational, civilized, and advanced society. At the same time, they recognize the challenges and complexities often inherent in doing so. They strive never to think simplistically about complicated issues, nor too critically of simplistic issues, and always consider the basic human needs and wants of the greater community. Critical thinkers attempt to self-liberate the anecdote, while focused on what really motivates humans to strive for success and happiness.

Maslow explained the graduation of "needs" in every human-being with his "Human Behavior Pyramid." I don't want to get too technical with Maslow's theories, but the explanation of his pyramid will help drive a point home. At the bottom of his pyramid, Maslow suggested, were the basic needs of every man and woman. Those basic needs involve food, water, shelter, clothing, and air. Our basic needs describe our desire for simple survival. The next level up on the pyramid is instinctive needs. At this position on the pyramid, Maslow suggests that humans strive to satisfy our need for security, safety, employment benefits, and retirement. This position can be called our conditions of self-centeredness. The third level of the pyramid describes our emotional human needs. Once our basic needs and instinctive needs are met, we seek love and relationships with family, friends, and co-workers. At this third level, we become other-people-centered. The forth position is where we desire to fulfill our professional needs. We want to be recognized, rewarded, and promoted for our professional achievements. At this stage of the pyramid, men and women become very ego-centric. At the final stage at the very top of the pyramid, we strive to satisfy our ultimate need as humans. That need is ultimate fulfillment in our professional and personal lives. At this position, Maslow suggests that humans need to feel a strong sense of accomplishment. This is the very stage that provides the sense of self-actualization. Self-actualization is the ultimate need of man. Your position on the human behavior (needs) pyramid is normally predicated on the quality of your thinking and on how effective you are in deploying your thoughts the assist in achieving want you desire and need.

Critical thinking is essential to your personal and professional growth and performance. Your human behavior conforms to the degree to which you are able to satisfy your human needs at each position on the pyramid. Understand unequivocally the subjugating effect of the Maslow Human Behavior Pyramid on your happiness, well-being, and success. You can not free yourself from this pyramid. The pyramid describes the very basic human needs, and everyone is subjected to the human behavior associated with your current position on the pyramid. If you have not attained a level of self-actualization in your personal and/or professional life, then you are unhappy in your current circumstances. Your behavior will reflect your unhappiness. If you feel self-actualized at home or at work, but hollowness exists in your personal need to receive accolades from your spouse, siblings, parents, or children or in your professional need of receiving awards, recognition, and/or advancement in employment; then you are unsatisfied in your current situation. Your behavior will convey your dissatisfaction. To be completely happy within your situation, condition, and time; your human needs must be fulfilled at all levels.

If you could identify 20 billionaires, 18 of them would be experiencing some level of dissatisfaction at some level on the pyramid. Even in the life of a billionaire there can exists a vacuum of sort in his or her life as a result of personal or professional unhappiness or malcontentedness with himself or herself or with someone within their associations. Money tends to only satisfy our basic and instinctive needs (food, water, shelter, clothing, security, and safety). And remember that these need are at the bottom of the pyramid. No amount of money and no level of intellect can free you from the subjugation of the Human Behavior Basic Needs Pyramid. Critical thinking can assist you in understanding your position on the pyramid and help you determine the critical paths to fulfilling all of your human needs so you can provide yourself and all your associations with the opportunity to be as great as possible. The qualities of our lives are directly related to the qualities of our thoughts. Your thoughts aide you in satisfying your overall human need to feel self-actualized. Your critical thoughts will help you reach the top of the pyramid. Rich people and poor people are unhappy for the same basic reason. Their lives are unfulfilled at some position on the pyramid of human needs. Both can create a critical thinking ability and become fully inserted in the process of reaching the ultimate satisfying feeling that only comes when they have accomplished their ultimate goal; whatever their ultimate goal in life may be.

"As crucial and precious as the intellect is, it can become a refuge that hides and conceals emotional underdevelopment, and diminishes your ability to think critically."

—Dr. Cornel West, Hope on a Tightrope

Amassing tremendous amounts of wealth is not a precondition to thinking critically. Obtaining a Ph.D. from Harvard or Yale is not a precondition to thinking critically. Fervently loving the truth and compassionately committing to inquiry are the only preconditions to critical thinking. And where there exists love and a compassionate commitment, there also exist success and fulfillment. To succeed in your life's endeavors, you must love fervently what you strive to bring into existence; you must compassionately commit every ounce of your life to bringing that thing into being, and critical thinking will provide the how, what, when, where, and why.

An Argument for Critical Thinking:

Is there a potential problem with thinking? Everyone thinks. It is human nature to do so. The problem is how and to what degree or level we think. Left unexamined, thinking leans toward distortion, prejudice, partiality, biasness, simplicity, or down-right ignorance. But the quality of life depends on the quality of thought. The quality of our products depends on the quality of thought that went into the production process. Excellent thoughts generate high quality products. Simple thoughts produce simple results. Critical thinking represents the highest order of all human faculties and must be intellectually and systemically developed. And again, an excellent system will generate thought of the highest quality.

THE ACT OF THINKING: Critical thinking is a modality of thinking (scientific thinking, mathematical thinking, historical thinking, anthropological thinking, economic thinking, moral thinking, and/or philosophical thinking) in reference to or about any subject, information, situation, condition, time, issue, or problem in which the thought generator strives to advance the quality of his or her thinking ability by intellectually and deliberately manipulating universal structures inherent in thinking and subjecting the structures to intellectual standards in divisions of subject matter clarity, accuracy, precision, consistency, relevancy, sound evidence, good reasons, depth, breadth, complexity, simplicity, and fairness.

THE RESULT OF CRITICAL THINKING: A Systemically Well-developed Critical Thinker will:

•Inject critically important questions, nuances, and problems; formulating them clearly and unequivocally;

•Obtain and evaluate relevant information and data, utilizing "out-of-the-box" ideas, frameworks, and concepts to effectively interpret the information and data, and deliver intellectual conclusions and solutions; examining the conclusions and solutions for relevancy and reliability based on established criteria and rigorous standards;

•Think with an open-minded intelligence in an unorthodox manner within alternative systemic thought processes; organizing, and examining assumptions; conclusions, and consequences of alternative viewpoints and frames of references.

•Communicate efficiently and effectively with all others to ensure the best possible self-liberating solutions to problems, complex or not so complex, are produced; and

•Generate a sense of self-actualization within and incite others to think as well.

Thinking is the master key that will unlock the doors to the pathways of success in both your personal and professional life. If you realize nothing else, realize that you can not become the greatest You without first thinking your greatest thoughts. Rhonda Bryne, in *The Secret,* states it this way: *"When you think about what you want, and you emit that frequency, you cause the energy of what you want to vibrate at that frequency and you bring it to You! As you focus on what you want, you are changing the vibration of the atoms of that thing, and you are causing it to vibrate to You. The reason you are the most powerful transmission tower in the Universe is because you have been given the power to focus your energy through thoughts and alter the vibrations of what you are focused on, which then magnetically draws it to you."* Rhonda Bryne clearly explains why there can only be one Jack Welch, one General Electric Company, one Bill Gates, one Microsoft Corporation, one Michael Jordan, one Chicago Bulls, one Oprah Winfrey, one Harpo Studios, one Tiger Woods, one Muhammad Ali, and only one You. The vibrations of your thoughts generate a unique frequency. That unique frequency causing the thing your thoughts are focused on to vibrate at the exact same frequency. Your frequency is unique to only you. It is like a secret code that no one else knows but you. It is like Cinderella's slipper. Only her foot could fit that slipper. Because of the uniqueness of our individually and secretively coded frequency, only we can control the things we have caused to vibrate at our frequency by focusing our thoughts on those things. Only Jack Welch could have produced the General Electric that he did. Every CEO who futilely attempted to produce another General Electric at his or her company discovered that to be fact. Only Michael Jordan could produce the frequency to cause six NBA Championships to vibrate magnetically to the Chicago Bulls franchise. Bills Gates is the only human on this planet with thoughts that could have produced Microsoft. Tiger Woods is the only professional Golfer with the thinking frequency to draw unto himself what Tiger Woods draws to his life and will draw to his life in the future. You are the only person who can generate the necessary frequency with your thoughts to bring the things you want to you. You don't have to be like Mike to be great. You just have to think your own great thoughts, and you will be uniquely great based on the vibrations you emit and the things your unique frequency magnetically draws to you.

Critical thinking must be systemically developed to produce a consistent frequency. Muhammad Ali did not become the "Greatest" simply by sitting at home on his sofa thinking he wanted to be the Greatest. His thinking was systemic, and as a result he developed a critical thinking process that delivered resolve. He systemically created a thought frequency that magnetically drew greatness to himself. He created a dimension for systemic critical thinking that managed and maintained his unique frequency, thus drawing to him all that he accomplished. This dimension created a systemic approach to Muhammad Ali's training and fight management. He did not just show up and fight. Ali trained like no other boxer in history. Ali would start out a training day by jogging until he was completely exhausted. He would then train on the punching bags and other boxing ring apparatuses until he could go no longer. Then at the very point of absolute physical fatigue and mental fragility unthinkable to most athletes, he would step into the boxing ring and start sparring. With his systemic training regimen, Muhammad Ali knew beyond any shadow of doubt that he always had more physical stamina and mental toughness than his opponent. Many thought Ali was just a loud mouth with quick hands. Only a few knew of the system that provided the world with its greatest Heavy-Weight Boxing Champion. Thought produced the frequency that produced the storied history of the world's most recognized person. A dimension for systemic critical thinking will do the same for you. You must develop your own system. If not, a system will be provided for you, and it may not work to your favor.

"If you don't have the courage to think critically for yourself, then someone will do the thinking for you, offering nothing substantive for your life. People have a way of pressuring you into complacency and maybe even pushing you into downright wretchedness. Before long, you rationalize your situation and learn to depend on others to do your every thinking."

—Ronald T. Hickey

There are 10 dimensions for a systematic approach to critical thinking. The 10 dimensions are described below as a "Critical Thinking Management Plan." There is no set manner in which these 10 dimensions are approached, developed, and managed. Everyone's situation, condition, and time are unique. I have purposely avoided providing a cookie cutter plan because your systematic critical thinking management plan should look like no other. This is not a "one size fits all" book or program. In fact none are, even though there are many books and programs being advertised that tend to give the end user a very rigid model to deploy. The goal is to become the greatest You. You have to avoid the temptation of allowing others to think for you. You decrease yourself and develop a crippling dependency when you become complacent with accepting the thoughts of others as the law of the land and as the only manner to address a particular situation. As Russell Simmons would encourage, "Do You!" With that said, each dimension is discussed below in brief to provide some initial thoughts that may exist as fertilization for impregnating your own thoughts on the matter. But make no mistake; this should be your management plan that addresses your own unique needs. The quality of the critical thinking management plan you give birth to will be predicated on the quality of the thought that goes into producing it. You may even discover that your situation could benefit from additional dimensions developed with the exercise of thinking critically. Be courageous, and if you live with a compassionate commitment to your circumstance, your plan will be perfect for you.

CRITICAL THINKING MANAGEMENT PLAN:

STRONG LEADERSHIP: For any system to be successful, strong leadership is a must. All great leaders encourage critical thinking by everyone in the organization or on the team. No one person is greater than the sum total of ideals, intellect, talent, ambition and knowledge of the group of individuals. We can continue the debate of whether great leaders are born or developed through training, experience, and education. But every great family, championship team, and/or successful business requires a great leader with strong leadership abilities; and that is not debatable. So if you are in a position of leadership, develop into a strong leader; and remember, you must possess love and compassionate commitment for your cause and your people before you can lead them to unprecedented levels of success. If your leader does not have a love ethic or commit every ounce of herself or himself to you and your cause, your leader will only have the ability to command. Commanding without leadership produces low performance, misguided intentions, discouraging thought, dissention, and arrogance. Strong Leadership is the first dimension to develop in your systematic critical thinking management plan. Without it, nothing will be successful.

THINKING FOCUSED TRAINING: This is a very critical dimension. Just like world-class athletes train to ensure their bodies are well conditioned to accomplish the feats of great athleticism, you must train your mind to produce world-class critical thoughts so you can accomplish the feats of greatness that you so desire. Use Muhammad Ali as an example and develop a way of training that focuses on thinking as he did. Muhammad Ali would think of things he could utilize outside the ring to defeat his opponents before they ever stepped into the boxing ring. Start considering your situations outside of the normal spaces in which you deal with them. If you do so with commitment to intellectual thought, love, and compassion; you will begin to develop resolve that can be deployed prior to engaging the situation. An important note to make here is that the mind needs rest just as the physical body does. The more you learn to rest your mind, with meditation being one manner of doing so, the more productive your mind will be in producing critical thought and important answers for your life and associations.

Thinking Focused Operations: Encourage everyone in your association to provide valuable input to increase the quality of operational output. Even in your family, encourage each person to think and provide answers to problems facing the family. Each of my children taught me that there is only one expert when it comes to solving personal issues. The expert is the person having the issue. Never assume you know a person better than she knows herself or he knows himself. Always ask for input from everyone directly involved in the situation or operation. That is the cornerstone of Thinking Focused Operations. The Targeted Performance Matrixes dimension discussed below will provide feedback into how well you are doing in this area. Proper training and practice in critical thinking should produce some tremendous results. The key here is to know what is "proper" training. So remember: Proper Preparation Producing Peak Performance. Focus your operations on thinking the 5 P's.

Talent Management Plan: Talent Management was discussed in detail in Chapter 3. Review the chapter if necessary. No additional information is offered in this summation. But please, don't ignore this dimension. A chapter in the book is dedicated to this subject. The fact that an entire chapter further discusses talent management in detail conveys just how important this dimension is to your overall success and happiness. The inability to assess, recruit, retain and manage talent is a primary reason we fail in many of our endeavors. While failure itself is not a calamity, not understanding why you experience failure is a definite calamity. Frame this dimension with care and fortitude.

Targeted Performance Matrixes: You should never neglect developing a means by which to evaluate and drive performance. Provide all of your operations with specific goals and performance targets. Charts, graphs, and performance matrixes are excellent means of visualizing and communicating performance goals. I am a big user and a big proponent of targeted performance goals. I even use such matrixes for the costs of utility and bathroom supplies at home. If you are not meeting your performance goals, then bring everyone to the table and get input into why not and into how you are going to meet your goals next month. This will provide everyone with the opportunity to think in a problem solving manner and come up with solutions. This process of problem solving becomes a critical dimension in your personal and professional lives as demand on limited resources, costs of continued operations, and the costs of every day living continue to increase every year. In any operation, you should be able to account for how you are spending valued resources. Additionally, this dimension informs you of the quality of your overall critical thinking management plan. If critical thinking has or has not produced quality in any of your other dimensions, targeted performance goals will clearly showcase the situation. There is an enormous amount of literary work available in the marketplace and bookstores that will provide valuable insight on how to develop a targeted performance based matrix system for your given situation. Choose wisely.

Effective Communications: Critical thinking becomes negligent as a tool for betterment if you are ineffective in communicating your thoughts; for what good are ideas if you are unable to communicate or deploy them? This dimension encourages you to develop a framework for seamlessly communicating across all the other dimensions. One hand must know what the other is doing at all times for the two hands to be successful. Have you ever had the pleasure of observing the perfect communication between Jerry Rice and Joe Montana during a two minute drive when the San Francisco 49ers needed a touchdown to win? Talk about a well defined dimension for critical thinking management,

Bill Walsh was an expert. And his communication style was the catalyst that made everything work in tandem and deliver seamless communication at every aspect of the game.

Technology provides a plethora of mediums and means for communicating. Additionally, there are a number of traditional manners of effective communication that lend themselves to a variety of situations. Given your unique situation, develop, as Bill Walsh did, an effective means of communicating with everyone in all of your associations. With so many options available, one is hard-pressed to give a valid and acceptable reason for poor communication, or the lack of communication all together. I understand that everyone presents his or her own personal style of communication, and some work better than others. Just ensure everyone clearly understands the thoughts involved in your plan. If not, the team will struggle to succeed. Communication does not have to be costly to be effective. Communication tends to be the most effective among those who have an intimate knowledge of one another.

Money is better spent on training and other resources to help team members develop a more intimate knowledge of who their teammates are, instead of building a costly communication system that never requires personal contact. Imagine a relationship with a spouse that did not involve physical contact. With today's technology, you could communicate effectively in many areas. But would the relationship succeed? If you know your teammates, you will learn how best to communicate effectively. Again, there is no cookie cutter for communication. Jerry Rice and Joe Montana developed their own model, and you knew when their communication was off. It was starkly obvious. Likewise, you knew when their communication was perfect. Both have Super Bowl Championship rings to attest to their perfect communication with one another. Develop an effective means of communicating critical thought within your teams. Do so, and the catalyst for success will support your every operation.

SUCCESS PATTERNS DEVELOPMENT: Developing patterns for success will be discussed in greater detail in the following chapter, Chapter 5. Patterns save us valuable time and resources and provide for consistency in the quality of our operations. If I discovered a successful path to work that saved me more time and money than any other path, then it would be prudent for me to take that path each time I traveled to work if the path was available. It would not make much sense for me to map out a new direction to work each morning. I could not predict the quality or consistency of my commute to any reasonable degree. The same concept applies to our every day personal and professional lives. Things go much more smoothly when we develop successful patterns and follow them each time we have the opportunity. This dimension supports understanding what works and why in your operations and what does not work and why in your operations. Both are discussed in detailed in subsequent chapters. But success patterns also become vitally important when operations do not go as planned. If you have been following a pattern, then you will know immediately where the problem occurred. This lends itself to troubleshooting the problem. If you know what works, then you will be able to quickly determine why it did not work on a particular day or in a particular situation.

I normally leave home every morning at 7:00 AM, and my commute time to work is 25 minutes. If I leave home at 7:15 AM, and my commute time to work is 40 minutes because the later start time results in driving slower due to heavier traffic congestion; I can evaluate my patterns and determine that the time I start my commute influences my arrival time at work. I understand that this is a simplified explanation, but when you have established great patterns for success, you have also simplified the process of evaluating failures. Chapter 5 will discuss how to develop such patterns.

SOLUTIONS DELIVERY SYSTEMS: Developing solutions as a result of critical thinking without a delivery system is equivalent to building an Aircraft Carrier on dry land that is 1000 miles from the nearest deep water channel to an ocean. What's the point? Did you build the Aircraft Carrier simply because you could? Do you plan to think critically and never deliver your solutions to any problem? What would be the point? Don't do it simply because you can. Do it with a purpose in mind, and the delivery system will develop itself. There are many great critical thinkers locked up behind prison walls all over the world. Many of their solutions to critical problems will, more than likely, never be paired with a delivery system that could deploy such critical thinking to the world. As prisoners, with their liberty denied, their thinking valued thoughts is equivalent to building Aircraft Carriers on dry land. The thoughts will never float because the ocean is not available. Don't wait until you are locked up in the prisons of your mind or disenfranchised from the operations you are associated with before you begin thinking. Think freely, think often, and think with a purpose in mind. And love the people you are in association with enough to share your valuable insight. The delivery system becomes crucial if resolve is to occur.

THINKING IMPROVEMENT PLAN: To become better at something, you must continually think improvement. It does not matter how great you think it is. My mother always told me to never stop trying to make my marriage better. She said my marriage will be healthy if that remained my approach. Improving your ability to think critically works in a similar manner. If you constantly strive to become a better thinker, you will never be a bad thinker, because you will harness the love for inquiry and develop an eternal passion for the truth. I developed an immediate love for the game of chess, even when I vaguely knew all the rules. Each time I played, I desired so much to become better at the game. I realized that I had to play chess players that were better at the game than I was, if I was to become better at the game. Challenge your critical thinking ability in like manner, and you will improve your thinking. Books by or about great thinkers of history are a great way of providing such challenges for the mind. You should always reach beyond what is easily in your grasp if you wish to grow beyond and outside of yourself.

RELEVANT CRITERIA: Within this dimension you must define the criteria for what will be considered relevant to your given situation. You can not simply ask someone or some organization what they would do if they were you. They are not you. Understand that only you can truly ascertain your situation from the inside. There is no book written where you will find within its pages the answers to all your problems. You must also define what will be the criteria for need in critical thinking, progress in critical thinking, success in critical thinking, and how well you are managing your system for critical thinking.

THE FOURTH CHALLENGE:

Create a Framework for Critical Thinking

1. Develop a plan for managing the 10 Dimensions of Systematic Critical Thinking Management.

a. Strong Leadership

b. Thinking Focused Training

c. Thinking Focused Operations

d. Talent Management Plan

e. Targeted Performance Metrics

f. Effective Communications

g. Success Patterns Development

h. Solutions Delivery Systems

i. Thinking Improvement Plan

j. Relevant Criteria

2. Read the following books:

    a. *The World is Flat*, Thomas L. Friedman

    b. *The Metamorphosis*, Frantz Kafka

    c. *The Soul of a Butterfly,* Muhammad Ali

    d. *Good to Great*, Jim Collins

    e. *The Halo Effect*, Phil Rosenzweig

    f. *The Goal*, Eliyahu M. Goldratt

    g. *Walden*, Henry David Thoreau

    h. *The Secret*, Rhonda Byrne

    i. *The Tibetan Book of Living and Dying*, Sogyal Rinpoche

    j. *The Audacity of Hope*, Barrack Obama, 44thPresident of the United States

    k. *Do You!*, Russell Simmons

    l. *Hope on a Tightrope*, Dr. Cornell West

3. List 3 personal beliefs this book has changed.

4. List 3 new personal beliefs as a result of this book.

5. Develop your new beliefs and values. Think more.

6. Live life more abundantly. Read more.

CHALLENGE FIVE

DEVELOP PROCESS PATTERNS FOR SUCCESS

"There are no secrets to success, but there are pathways. Just as you can not walk upon sand without leaving a path of footprints behind, you can not succeed at anything without leaving a distinct pathway to that success behind. Such a pathway becomes a pattern for the entire world to follow. The decision to follow belongs to the individual."

—Ronald T. Hickey

Everything in life is a process. Life itself is a process, and for any process to be successful, some very specific steps or actions have to be taken. Those steps or actions identify what was required to complete the process in the manner in which success was achieved in the given situation. The steps or actions taken may not prove successful in another situation with totally different circumstances. But with a given situation, certain steps or actions will prove to be the ones required for success. I had a dear old aunt that lived to be 94 years old. I often wondered about the many right decisions she had to make in her life to live to be 94 years old, given that so many of us don't live to be half that age. I would ask myself that question in a humble inquiry to ascertain if there were some secrets to good living that would guarantee longevity. While Aunt Eleanor was not a perfect human, no human is, the steps and actions she chose in her life were precisely the ones she had to make and undertake to live 94 years on this earth. Aunt Eleanor was perfectly healthy up until she fell and broke her hip, six months before she passed away. Aunt Eleanor was a devout Christian woman. Auntie died penniless because she gave what ever she had to anyone she deemed to be in need. If a person attempted to follow in the footsteps of my aunt, those are just a few of the footsteps he or she would have to take. Aunt Eleanor's life was a process. She had a successful process for 94 years. How many processes can we identify that were or have been successful for 94 years? Not many! Now, if I want to live a successful life for as long as Auntie did, then I need to look closer and more purposely at the things she did right and that made her life process such a successful journey. If I looked close enough and analyzed enough, I would be able to trace patterns Aunt Eleanor left in the fabric of society. I would be able to observe patterns she left in the sands of time. I would be able to develop process patterns for successful living from analyzing my aunt's success in experiencing longevity on this earth. All that I would discover about my aunt's life would not necessary be useful or applicable to my given situation and circumstance. She was born in 1914, and I was born in 1964. The 50 years that separate our births define situations, conditions, and times that affect the results of success in our lives, based on a particular action she would take and that I would take. But nevertheless, I could develop a process pattern for a successful life based on the footprints she left behind for me to follow.

In life, many successful people establish process patterns for success that can be identified, developed, and implemented by another. Successful businesses and organizations leave footprints in the sand that can be followed as a road map to success. The largest employer in the state of California is the Chevron Corporation. Chevron originally formed as a company under the name of Pacific Coast Oil Company in 1879. The name Chevron was adopted in 1984. While the names have changed several times over more than 130 years, the company has remained the same: very SUCCESSUL, even during the Great Depression. A company as large, and as successful, as Chevron has left many footprints in the oil and natural gas industry sands. The oil and natural gas companies that have chosen to follow Chevron's footprints have been very successful as well. My father-in-law retired from Chevron after 37 years of service. He retired in 2000. Joseph often boasts that in the 37 years he worked for the Chevron Corporation he was never laid-off, "not even for a day." This is a tremendous statement coming from my father-in-law when you realize he is an African-American with only a high school formal education. The statement is even more tremendous when you realize that a company as large and mature as the Chevron Corporation never had to lay-off a blue-collar worker with a limited education at any time between 1965 and 2000. Such a statement is a definite indication of a company that has experienced much success. Furthermore, such a company has imprint some very distinctive footprints in the sand. Those footprints provide the very patterns for success for any company willing to do as the Chevron Corporation has for more than 130 years.

Each person or each company can look closer and more purposely at the things my Aunt Eleanor did or the Chevron Corporation has done that made for such successful journeys. If you observe a person, family, team, organization, or company that is experiencing the degree and manner of success you so fervently desire; look closer and more purposely at the "things" that person, family, team, organization, or company is doing right that is responsible for the process that accounts for success. The "things" are threads that weave the tapestry of the patterns. Success can be predicated on these patterns, and these patterns identify precisely the actions you can complete; or your family, team, organization, or company can also complete, to be successful. You can go through the painstaking process of developing your own process patterns for success; but why suffer such an ordeal and plethora of trials and errors, wasting precious time and efforts, and lane changes and redirections in your life while still having no guarantee for success and happiness if you don't have to? Follow the patterns and step into the footprints of those successful giants who have come before you.

The idea behind developing process patterns for success from the examples provided by others is that we should avoid reinventing the wheel and repeating unnecessary mistakes. While I am a staunch advocate of not reinventing the wheel, I am also a proponent of understanding the unique terrain upon which I must navigate the wheel. Just as the 50 years that separated my aunt and I prescribed that I had to take into account the differences in our circumstances when I considered what made her life so successful, we have to take our given situations into account when we are working with someone else's or some other organization's pattern for success. When I go out to practice my golf swing after watching a David Leadbetter interactive DVD movie, I have to remind myself of the physical limitations my 44 year old body presents. While I can definitely use the information provided by David Leadbetter as a process pattern for a more successful golf swing, I also have to take into account my bad back, my stiff neck, my weak knee, and all else that hinders me from swinging a golf club like a 21 year old. I do have a successful golf swing. My swing is not successful because I swing my golf clubs just as David Leadbetter instructs. My swing is successful because I start with the instructions David Leadbetter suggests for a perfect golf swing, and I apply the information to my given situation and circumstances. I do not swing golf clubs perfectly, but without the process pattern for a successful golf swing provided by one the world's best golf swing coach, I would not be as successful in the game of golf as I am.

Becoming successfully efficient at the task at hand in as timely a manner as possible is the primary purpose for developing process patterns for success. The patterns will exist as instructions to save you time, energy, and resources. The patterns will exist as checkpoints to inform you if you are on the right path or off in left or right field. The process patterns will exist as train tracks as you engine yourself like a locomotive through the wilderness of life. Process patterns for success will guide you each step of the way as you set out on your journey to become as great as you can be. Don't start the trip until you have the path all mapped out. If success is the final destination of the trip, process patterns are the map.

"Many people work hard to climb the ladder to success, and suddenly find that their ladder is leaning up against the wrong wall."

—Don Hutson, Co-Author of The Contended Achiever

The selection of patterns to follow must be done with extreme care and forethought. You want to make sure that your selection will deliver the intended results. A pattern, in and of itself, can not provide guarantees for success. A particular pattern intrinsically is designed to provide the portal to a specific end, and the utilization of that particular pattern will ensure the associated specific end is consistently realized. Process patterns can ensure you are either consistently successful or consistently unsuccessful; depending on the pattern and the end associated with the pattern. A person should not harbor any real expectations for becoming a healthy, wealthy, and wise 90 year old man or woman, if he or she has been traveling the pathway of a drug addicted, unemployed high school drop-out. That particular pattern will consistently prove to be unsuccessful for many positive goals in life. A company, organization, professional team, or family should have no real expectations for any form of success while utilizing process patterns that have been proven to only result in destructive conditions. I recall one of the first news articles I read about Michael Jordan after he joined the Chicago Bulls NBA franchise as a rookie basketball player fresh out of the University of North Carolina. This particular article conveyed information that suggested Michael Jordon had joined his teammates following a game at some post-game function. When Michael arrived at the post-game function, he observed his teammates engaged in activities that were counterproductive to them becoming a winning NBA Championship franchise. Michael supposedly left the function immediately. At some time shortly after this event, Michael met with team officials and informed the officials that the Chicago Bulls NBA franchise was not on the path to a NBA Championship; in fact, he informed the officials that the team was on a course that would only ensure that the Chicago Bulls would remain one of the worse teams in the NBA. Michael Jordan reminded the Chicago Bulls that he was there for one reason, and that one reason was to win championships. In his rookie year with the Chicago Bulls, Michael led the team in scoring, rebounding, assists, and steals. He was serious about winning and knew a pattern for success had to be developed. The team officials listened to Michael. The Chicago Bulls became very serious about winning and developed process patterns that would provide consistent winning. The process patterns the franchised had begun using in 1984 were promulgated in 1991, seven years later, when the Chicago Bulls won their first of six NBA Championships. Speaking of how the correct patterns can provide consistency for success, the Bulls won six championships in eight years. One of those years involved Michael Jordan temporarily retiring from the NBA. Now, that is consistency, and that is exactly what the right process pattern can deliver. Be the Michael Jordan of all of your associations. Identify and reject unequivocally destructive and counterproductive processes that provide nothing positive toward the successful end. Develop the correct process patterns for success in your endeavors that will consistently make you a winner. Commit your entire being to those correct processes and find yourself in championship contention year after year.

If you want to succeed at anything, you must commit to patterns that are proven to result in the success you seek. For success to be consistent, the goal should be only to develop process patterns that are proven to deliver the success you are out to achieve. The river otter could never be successful at building a dam in the river if he patterned his committed activities after the activities of the tree squirrel building a nest in a tree. Follow the footprints that lead to where you wish to go. Infidelity does not lead to a wonderful and happy relationship with your spouse. Fiscal irresponsibility does not lead to financial independence. Mismanagement of the employee talent pool does not lead to 130 plus years of success as a corporation. Engaging in post-game illegal activities does not lead to championships. The intention here is not to imply that fidelity alone leads to a happy relationship or financial responsibility will guarantee you riches and wonders. Fidelity is simply one thread of the pattern one would expect to find in the fabric of a healthy relationship between a husband and his wife. Couples that continue to try and make a relationship work when there is continuous infidelity damaging the emotional health of the relationship are driving themselves insane. They keep doing the same things over and over and expecting different results. If you find yourself committed to engaging in a situation that has been unfavorable for a substantial amount of time; unless significant positive changes are developed and committed to, you should have no expectations for the situation getting better. On the other hand, if you commit yourself and your associations to engaging in activities known to deliver success in your particular endeavor, whether the endeavor is personal or professional, you will surely succeed. The level of commitment I am referring to is in no manner or form small by any measure; it is devotion. If we have devotion, total faith and commitment, to our path to success, a monstrous momentum will derive from our unwavering determination to achieve, succeed, and become great. Soon we will notice that boundaries are widened in the moments, obstacles become fewer each day, and confidence increases exponentially. Our path magically becomes very vivid and free of most hazards. Our steps appear clearly ordered in a straight line fashion. Nothing will deter us from our purpose, no matter what the challenges are that we must face. The level of devotion I am referring to requires more than just simply staying the course. Fortitude and attitude must be of the appropriate pedigree. Our entire being must be completely and unequivocally focused upon our single endeavor. This level of devotion requires the total sum of all that is within us. If we converge all that is within us in a united system with all that is outside of us in our commitment to this singular point of reference, then success will become intimately a part of our every existence.

As a rookie in 1984, Michael Jordan immediately realized that the Chicago Bulls would not evolve into a championship franchise without the franchise committing to the implementation of some significant positive changes in how the team operated. Michael Jordan knew that the entire Chicago Bulls franchise had to devote itself to one singular endeavor: winning NBA championships. In the same year of Michael's rookie season, famed auto industry legend Lee Iacocca co-authored his autobiography with William Novak. Lee Iacocca's story of how he was fired from the Ford Motor Corporation without good cause by Henry Ford wanes only to his storied success in turning the troubled Chrysler Corporation around in the early 1980's. Lee Iacocca understood the level of devotion associated with rescuing an ailing automaker from bankruptcy and the doom of shutdown. His understanding of the level of required commitment to changing how Chrysler was operating when he took over is the primary reason he was able to successfully get all required entities to devote to saving Chrysler, including the United States federal government. In his 1984 autobiography, Lee Iacocca warns the American people that, *"... we've got to make some basic decisions. Unless we act soon, we're going to lose both steel and autos to Japan by the year 2000. And worst of all, we will have given them up without a fight."* What Lee Iacocca was saying is that the automobile industry and many other industries in American business had leaderships that were running their companies in manners that would not allow these American companies to remain competitive or in existence, without some significant positive changes in the way in which they operated. In his approach to a very serious sitaution, Lee Iacocca did what he could to impress fervently upon the minds of other companies and their leaderships to devote to change or prepare to go out of business.

We know the way of steel companies in America. Bust! Steel manufacturing companies did not even come close to making it to the year 2000. And here we stand in 2009 with the American automobile manufacturing companies begging for a stimulus package from the Unites States Congress and on the brink of annihilation by Japanese automakers. Lee Iacocca forewarned the industry. America's Big 3 automakers; Ford, General Motors, and Chrysler have been doing the same things over and over for about 20 to 30 years and expecting different results, and now it seems a bit insane for them to be going to the federal government for a financial bailout when they have refused to make significant positive changes in their operations. Unless the Big 3 American automakers develop and devote, total faith and commitment, to some proven process patterns for success, no amount of financial assistance will guarantee their existence as viable American corporations. What's really worth focusing in on about the situation involving the American automobile industry is that the Japanese automobile makers have left some very deep and distinctive footprints in the sands of the automobile industry. Ford, General Motors, and Chrysler have had ample opportunity to develop proven process patterns for successful automobile making and automobile industry operations by just simply patterning themselves after the Japanese models.

I have heard the arguments concerning the differences in the American workforce and the Japanese workforce. My business interests have afforded me the privilege of observing the Japanese workforce up close and personally while I was employed with Tyco International, Ltd. While I believe the differences in the two workforces definitely factor into the equations, I don't believe the factor is as great as the American public is lead to believe. Toyota took over an automobile manufacturing plant in Fremont, California that had been previously owned and operated by General

Motors for years. General Motors was not successful in its automobile manufacturing at the plant in Fremont, California. Toyota is highly successful in its automobile manufacturing in the same plant utilizing the same American workforce that GM employed at the plant. The difference in the two degrees of successes experienced in the plant by the two separate automobile companies is attributed to the Toyota leadership commitment to totally different process patterns for success within the plant operations. Toyota's patterns are designed for optimum success in the automobile industry. Are your patterns designed for optimum success in your endeavors? If you find that you have been engaged in the same activities time and time again without experiencing any advancement toward your desired level of success, don't subject yourself any longer to insanity. Find new patterns to follow. Look to the leader in your areas of interest, and extrapolate the process applicable to your situation. Devote your being to this new process, and success will find you.

No process pattern can guarantee peak performance 100% of the time. Success has its peaks and valleys, but proven patterns will increase your success rate to a predictable level. You may even fail on occasion, but stick to what has made you successful. You will experience victory far more often than you experience defeat. Your success will depend heavily on your ability in identifying the right pattern and knowing when to switch paths when presented with a crossroad. Knowing which path to take when presented with such options can be a challenge. A clear understanding of your unique circumstances and your established goals will assist in making the right decision. Avoid looking for answers in all the wrong places, and despite your best intentions, this is not always avoidable. All forms of literature, from published books and popular magazine articles to trade journals from well-known leaders and consultants are some of the more common places searched for the footprints and road maps to successful careers and relationships. These sources of information can be of great value if employed appropriately. Just keep in mind that there is no one road to success. There is no one book that will answer everyone's problems. There are more books authored on success and achievement, leadership and career management, and personal growth and self-help just in the past decade than one could possibly read in a reasonable amount of time. The joy of the journey is experienced within your personal engagement of the process, not within the literary pages written by others.

Well, one may ask, "Why don't the great books by the great minds always provide the right answers?" Well, because life is far too random; situations are far too varying; and conditions are far too unpredictable. No one person can speak to all the issues facing the almost 7 billion inhabitants of planet earth, much less convey his or her thoughts very easily on the pages of a book in such a manner that the answers to everyone's problems are expressed between the front and back covers of the book. In looking for patterns for success don't assume someone else's pathways to success are going to deliver the results you expect for your given conditions. Successful people are successful because they effectively discover and deploy patterns that work consistently in a variety of situations. Successful people are successful not because they are exceptional in any way, but because they are disciplined and devoted in their deployment of the ordinary patterns that have made many before them successful. Find the patterns that will deliver what you desire and deploy them with great devotion.

"Champions are champions not because they do anything extraordinary but because they do the ordinary things better than anyone else."

—Chuck Knoll, (retired) Coach, Pittsburgh Steelers

The key to capturing unprecedented achievements on a consistent basis is to locate the pattern that best addresses your particular needs. If we can learn what has worked repeatedly in the past, then we can emulate those successes and avoid our own failures. A single, one-size-fits-all, process for success does not exist! The elements associated with each problem are as unique as the individual person, family, team, company, or organization. There is no master plan; so stop going to garage sales buying old paintings hoping to find one concealed within the canvass. Simply look for the footprints of ordinary men and women of the past who have done ordinary things in such a manner that signs left behind evidence the great successes of their great accomplishments. Follow those signs! Follow the signs and there you will find the pattern. Follow the pattern and there you will find the success. Understand that the pattern must be utilized in a manner that takes into account our own uniqueness. No two people will employ the same pattern in the same manner, but each person who employs patterns of success with devotion, total faith and commitment will advance his or her agenda.

THE FIFTH CHALLENGE:

Read Dr. Stephen Covey's inspirational book, *7 Habits of Highly Effective People.*

1. Conduct a "self-assessment" and identify your most successful achievements. Determine 7 success factors most often used in these achievements and list them.

2. Conduct an assessment of someone who is experiencing a level of success that you desire for yourself. Determine 7 success factors that this person most often used and list them.

3. Conduct an assessment of a family or relationship that is experiencing a level of success and happiness that you desire for your family and/or relationship. Determine 7 success factors that this family or relationship most often used and list them.

4. Conduct an assessment of a team that is similar to your team and is experiencing a level of success that you desire for your team. Determine 7 success factors that this team most often used and list them.

5. Conduct an assessment of a company in your given industry that is experiencing a level of success that you desire for your company. Determine 7 success factors that this company most often used and list them.

6. Conduct an assessment of an organization similar to your organization that is experiencing a level of success that you desire for your organization. Determine 7 success factors that this organization most often used and list them.

7. Consider all of the success factors listed above. Identify the 7 most consistent successor factors most often used. Devote, total faith and commitment, your entire being to these 7 success factors.

8. Continual career success comes from recognizing and implementing proven success patterns. In particular, patterns of other successful people, effectiveness, self-assessment, forecasts, and the patterns of social trends.

These patterns coupled with your individual talents and skills are the formula for your happiness and success. Patterns are the keys to a successful journey. The goal in developing patterns is to ensure you are not carrying any errors forward and your process delivers desired results each and every time.

I would like to end this chapter with a short passage from Tony Dungy's inspirational book, *Quiet Strength.* Tony Dungy had just been successful as the first African-American head coach to win a National Football League Super Bowl when his book was published. He previously coached under Chuck Knoll, Marty Schottenheimer, and Denny Green, respectively. The passage reads as follows: *"Denny knew that football, like life, is unpredictable, but it was our job to train the team to remain disciplined even in unusual situations. As I thought about how to prepare the Bucs to handle any situation we might face, I went back to some of Denny's tactics. Once we had become locked in on a schedule, he often created a disruption to that schedule just to see how guys would respond. During the preseason of my first year with the Vikings, Denny announced that we were going to Cleveland on the day of the game. He said we would get off the plane, head to the stadium, and play. This was unusual; most teams travel to an away game at least a day before the game- sometimes arriving even two days early if it's an especially long trip. But Denny wanted to see how the players would adjust- who would adapt and who couldn't. His larger point was that there were always going to be moments of adversity and confusion during a game or a season, and players either adjusted or they crumbled. He wanted to know as much as possible ahead of time about the innate character of his team. On that occasion, the players grumbled a little, then flew into Cleveland and beat the Browns 51-3."*

Know your innate character ahead of time. Be prepared for unusual situations, adversity, confusion, and the things that are beyond your control. Your path will not always be straight. Patterns will not always deliver. But if you stay the course and devote yourself to the patterns, you will prepare your innate character to handle the unexpected and the unknown. You will develop confidence that you can succeed in the face of adversity. With that said, let's go meet the sixth challenge!

CHALLENGE SIX

UNDERSTAND WHAT WORKS AND WHY IT WORKS

"Work is love made visible. And if you cannot work with love but only with distaste, it is better that you should leave your work and sit at the gate of the temple and take alms of those who work with joy."

—Kahlil Gibran

Understanding what works and why it works is starkly different than developing patterns that are proven to be successful. Patterns provide the "how to" step by step procedure for accomplishing something or for reaching your desired destination with a great deal of consistency and accuracy. Knowing how the process patterns work and why they work afford you the opportunity to truly evaluate the efficiency and productiveness of the details and internal workings of the step by step procedures. While the joy may be in the final product, true love for the work is developed in the details of knowing how things happen. There is much joy in making your significant other happy on special occasions, but the true love develops in the details of learning what works and why it works in making him or her happy on a daily basis. Understanding the details of any process you are associated with provides similar emotions. So, whatever you may be engaged in, the quantity and quality of your commitment will determine the degree of your understanding for how and why it works. This commitment to learning the details of the procedure will also provide for understanding problems with the step by step process and how to correct those problems. And you must love something to have a genuine interest in learning the intrinsic workings of its operation. To master the understanding of a thing is to love that thing enough to want to know exactly how that thing works. Essentially, process patterns are the operating manual that describes which buttons to push and when; and understanding what works, how it works, and why it works is the troubleshooting manual that describes the specific details of exactly what is happening systematically when pushing the buttons fails to produce the intended operation.

Once process patterns are developed that deliver desired results, understanding the reasons the patterns are successful or effective become vitally important in the event things do not work out as planned. And nothing works out as planned each and every time. What works and why is the brick and mortar of your operations. This knowledge is what bonds the foundation to everything else you build upon it. A business, organization, or team must know what they are doing and why if they are going to be successful. If a business sets a goal of generating one million dollars in revenue for the year selling widgets, the business must know more than just how to make widgets. The business must know how to make widgets in the most cost effective manner. The business has to know how to identify and access the widget market. In reaching their goal of one million dollars in revenue for the year, the business must know what works in all facets of the widget business and why if the business is to be successful. Without this broad perspective and equitable knowledge, the only business activity the company will be engaged in is warehousing widgets. Likewise, in personal relationships and team environments, you must understand the details of the inner workings of relationships and teamwork. If not, you will discover you are just going through the motions just for the paycheck or physical attention. True happiness results from self-actualization, not the paycheck or some fleeting emotion. Self-actualization derives from relationships, personal and professional, in which you are compelled to give your absolute best in ensuring its success. What compels you to such success and satisfaction is that insatiable desire to understand more and more about the relationship within which you are laboring.

Inevitably, all relationships and associations hit bumps in the road from time to time. Those bumps interrupt the natural or normal paths of an otherwise good relationship or team environment. If the natural or normal path is made unavailable by a series of unplanned events, knowing what makes the relationship work and why proves critical to your ability to right what has gone wrong. If the path of a good relationship is interrupted by dishonesty and mistrust, what works and why it works to rebuild honesty and trust will become the foundation for rebuilding the relationship. Without that knowledge, the relationship will surely meet its demise. If a team has tremendous talent but no chemistry, such as the 1976-1977 Philadelphia 76ers NBA basketball team, your team is always subject to unexpected defeat; as with the 1976-1977 76ers who lost the NBA Championship to a less talented team of Portland Trailblazers who did have better team chemistry. After losing the NBA championship tournament series again in 1980 and 1982, the Philadelphia 76ers labored incessantly to put a talented team together that had great chemistry amongst its players. The team added the presence of Moses Malone as the big man in the middle. As a result, Moses helped lead the 76ers to the promise land, and they won the 1982-1983 NBA Championship by sweeping the Los Angeles Lakers in four games. Understanding what it took to win a championship gave the franchise the ability to evaluate their players and to determine what the missing pieces were. Knowing what works and why was the foundation upon which the 76ers franchise built their championship NBA team. It is the foundation upon which all teams win championships. Process patterns for success will convey to a NBA team that you don't win championships without a talented big man in the middle. Knowing what works and why conveys that the big man in the middle is an integral ingredient of the foundation for winning a championship. Good team chemistry, great role players, talent in other critical positions, and a damn good coach are the building blocks of that foundation. And teams that have leaderships that understand why that works are the teams we are all familiar with because they are constantly winning or contesting for championships.

"Understanding how something works gives you opportunity in your circumstances. Understanding why something works gives you control over your circumstances."

—Ronald T. Hickey

Back eons ago when Atari was the big name in the electronic gaming industry, the engineers who developed the software for the game programs had the knowledge. They knew the how, what, and why of all the Atari products. When the Atari leadership refused to approve the game developers' request for greater financial compensation for their knowledge that produced the products that made Atari games the most sought after in the industry, the game developers simply refused to release new software for the game programs. Eventually, the engineers left Atari for other electronic gaming companies, and Atari became a thing of the past. The game developers controlled their circumstances because they had the knowledge, and that knowledge was power. Companies have become smarter since the glory days of Atari. Leadership has proprietary laws on their side, and the smart men and women who are the center of the company's success are handsomely rewarded. But the power of knowledge continues to rule the day and give the possessor of such knowledge control over his or her circumstances. In any organization; the person who knows the what, how, and why of the operations is so much more valuable to the organization than the individual who only knows how to follow established instructions. The software architect that develops a new computer software program for the company is much more valuable than the computer operator on the manufacturing floor who simply follows step-by-step production procedures for manufacturing the compact disc containing the software program. Understanding why is true knowledge. Knowledge is power, and that power gives you control over your circumstances.

Ask yourself, who has complete control over his or her circumstance at Microsoft and why? While this person may be the Chairperson and/or CEO of Microsoft, the Chairperson and CEO is not always the one with the what, how, and why knowledge that controls his or her circumstance. If you think this is always the case, you may want to re-visit the matter concerning why Carly Fiorina is no longer the CEO of Hewlett-Packard. Carly Fiorina had great ideas, but her ideas where not necessarily ideas embraced by certain members of the corporate board. She may have understood how, but not why, things were done at Hewlett-Packard, as they related to relationships with board members, and eventually had to come to terms with who had true control over the corporation. While you are considering Carly Fiorina's situation, you may want to consider your situations as well. If you find that you do not have control over your circumstances (personal, professional, and social) you may want to increase your knowledge base on what, how, and why within all endeavors you are currently engaged.

Learning to drive an automobile is an excellent example for understanding how the knowledge of knowing what, how, and why is the difference between having opportunity within a circumstance and having control over the circumstance. When my father taught me how to drive his old 1968 Ford Galaxy 500, he just taught me the very basics of driving. He taught me how to start the engine with the automobile in park and how to have my foot on the break when I move the transmission from park to reverse or drive. He taught me to slowly push down on the gas peddle initially and how to stay on my side of the road when driving. He also taught me how to slow down and signal before turning. I slowly learned the basics of driving and was allowed to drive alone after earning my driver's license. The basic "step-by-step" knowledge of how to drive gave me the opportunity in certain circumstances to drive myself from place to place without having to rely on someone else. Driving provided me greater independence as a teenager. That basic knowledge gave me opportunity in my circumstances.

My father was also a master automobile mechanic. He had the ability to completely dismantle an automobile engine and re-assemble the engine to perfect operating condition. As a result of having a master automobile mechanic as a father, I learned a tremendous amount about how an automobile operated and why some mechanical parts operated as they did. As fate, circumstance, and statistics would have it, I was approximately 100 miles from home one night driving from college in my mother's automobile. All of a sudden the lights started to get dimmer and dimmer as I was driving. I finally had to pull off the freeway due to having insufficient lighting to continue. But because I learned so much about vehicles from a master vehicle mechanic, I knew that the problem was more than likely caused by the alternator not working properly. Sure enough, when I checked I found a loose alternator wire. I tightened the wire. And also knowing that a bad alternator also results in the battery being drained, I summoned another motorist to "jumper" my car battery to give the vehicle the start it needed. Once the vehicle started, the alternator was able to perform its function to run the vehicle and also to recharge the battery. I eventually made it home safely. Understanding how the alternator worked and why gave me control over my circumstance. Instead of being stranded 100 miles from home, I was able to right what was wrong with the vehicle and continue on my journey. This identifies the ultimate purpose of understanding what works and why. This very intricate understanding in things, situations, and circumstances that you are engaged in allows you to make the necessary corrections when something goes wrong or when you get off path so you can continue your journey to success. Having advanced knowledge of how automobiles operate, and not just the basics, allowed me control over my circumstances. I was able to make the necessary mechanical adjustments to my vehicle so I could continue on and successfully make it home. Without the knowledge of how an automobile worked, my routine process pattern of traveling between home and college would have been seriously interrupted. I had traveled that I-75 freeway in Tennessee that traversed between my home town and my college town often. I knew the directions for a successful route home. That pattern and route was always successful until that one fateful night when things did not go as planned. Are you somehow stranded 100 miles from our destination because the routine that has faithfully delivered you safely in the past has been unexpectedly interrupted? Have you veered from the beaten path and can't find your way back? Are you confident that you were following accurate directions? What lack of knowledge has deterred you from moving on from your stranded conditions?

Do you have the advanced knowledge required to understand what will get things working again in your relationship with your spouse, siblings, children, or friends? Or are you just stranded midway between the town of happiness and the city of despair without the required knowledge of how to get yourself back on the pathways of success? Do you know enough about your spouse to make him or her happy? Do you know enough about your children, parents, or friends to be a positive influence in their lives?

Do you know why things are no longer working as planned in your employment situations with your co-workers, subordinates, and superiors? Or are you just marred in improbable and impossible situations that have no real potential for success? Do you have the education and training to be highly successful at work? Do you have the advanced knowledge that promotes you to the "go to person"?

Do you know why your teamwork environments are no longer winning environments with your teammates, coaches, and organizational leaders? Or are you just going through the motions somewhere between isolated wins and mounting failure? Do you know the strengths and weaknesses of your teammates? Do you know what will breathe the atmosphere of success back into the team environment?

Before you embarked upon a journey in an automobile you must know that your automobile needs not just a set of tires; but that the tires must be properly inflated, balanced, and of good thread depth. If the tires are not in such condition this would present certain risk to completing the path you plan to travel safely. Are you prepared for challenges in your personal relationships? Are you ready to adapt to changes in your employment? Have you gained the advanced knowledge required to troubleshoot the problems that materializes in life and in your process patterns? Whatever your personal or professional situation may be make sure you are completely prepared for the journey you have chosen to embark upon. If you have failed to prepare in any manner, you are subject to having your journey interrupted because of your poor preparation; and a major part of any preparation is possessing advanced knowledge of systems and processes involved in your endeavor so you understand how to react to adversity along the way. This advanced knowledge in professional disciplines, romantic relationships, and team building assists in keeping you on track when unplanned situations arise. Remember, once you have established your path to success; there are no short cuts to this success; just distractions, interruptions; and delays. Knowing how to properly deal with those unplanned events will determine the very quality of the journey.

Harnessing advanced knowledge of processes and not just the basics of the step-by-step routine provide for properly adjusting to anomalies in your life. Let us employ the example of a common anomaly of a blown fuse. I think most of us have had to deal with a blown fuse, either in our car, home, or place of employment. The purpose of a fuse in an electrical circuit is to protect components in the circuit from excessive current (electrical amperage) conditions that could damage the component and cause it to not operate as required. Typically the fuse is a very inexpensive device that protects very expensive components. Additionally, a fuse is installed in such a location and manner within the electrical circuit that allows for it to be more easily replaced than other components. So when the fuse blows, we all understand the fuse must be replaced for the system to work. Every fuse has a current rating. All components in an electrical circuit are designed for a particular current rating. So when the fuse blows, the fuse must be replaced with a properly rated fuse. If we replace the blown fuse with an improperly rated fuse we potentially expose the components of the electrical circuit to current conditions that exceed what the components are rated for. The installation of an improperly rated fuse could result in very expensive repair costs. The destruction could result in excessive downtime of the system itself. This downtime could cost a company large amounts of money. Deadlines may not be met. The process you are engaged in may experience unnecessary distractions, interruptions, and delays. So when we decide on a fix for a problem that has found its way into our lives, as with replacing a fuse, the fix must be the proper fix. If we select an improper fix, the fix could cause major and catastrophic damages to our operations, teams, and families. Understanding what works and why helps us to understand how to properly correct a wrong. Understanding what works and why prevents us from using a sledge hammer to kill flies.

"You can eliminate mistakes by sticking to what you fully understand. Focusing on what you know provides an atmosphere of confidence in your work and promotes a foundation for growth. You can not get better at something until you understand what you are doing right and why you are doing it right. Without understanding this, success is only a matter of luck; and failure is simply a matter of time."

—Ronald T. Hickey

The Ukrainian Chernobyl Reactor Plant was a four-reactor nuclear reactor plant centrally located between what was then known as Belarus, Ukraine, and the Soviet Union of Russia. On April 25, 1986, prior to a routine shutdown, the reactor crew at Chernobyl-4 began preparing for a test to determine how long the turbines would continue to spin and supply power following a loss of main electrical power supply. This test was being conducted despite the fact that these reactors were known to be very unstable at low power settings due to a flawed design. A series of interruptions in the test caused the reactor to be in this unstable low power condition for an extended period of time. Additionally, operator actions, including the disabling of protective automatic shutdown mechanisms, preceded the attempted test early on April 26, 1986. As flow of coolant water diminished, power output increased. When the operator moved to shut down the reactor from its unstable condition arising from previous errors, a peculiarity of the design caused a dramatic power surge. The fuel elements ruptured and the resultant explosive force of steam lifted off the cover plate of the reactor, releasing radioactive fission products to the atmosphere. A second explosion threw out fragments of burning fuel and graphite from the core and allowed air to rush in, causing the graphite moderator to burst into flames. Approximately 50 deaths are attributed to this nuclear reactor accident. The Chernobyl nuclear reactor accident is a great reminder to the world of what can happen when you don't have complete understanding of your operations. Chernobyl was an accident that could have and should have been prevented. If the operators had not disabled the automatic protection that would have shutdown the reactor prior to any explosions, this incident would have never happened; at least not on April 26, 1986. I was actually working as a nuclear engineer in the United States Navy at the time of this incident. After learning of what the initial reports offered as the cause, I took more seriously the power in understanding what works and why. The Chernobyl Nuclear Power Plant Operators turned the computer control off to override a protection feature during a testing operation and then did not know how to manually operate the reactor systems when the need arose. Reports suggest that the operators were poorly trained and had only a basic understanding of nuclear theory and an even less understanding of the particular design of the Chernobyl reactors. I am aware that nuclear theory can be a challenge to understand, but I think this incident clearly makes the case for how important it is to fully understand what you are engaged in. Have you ever heard someone say, "I know just enough to be dangerous"? Basic knowledge can get you into trouble. Advanced knowledge keeps you out of trouble. The lack of proper training causes simple mistakes that could result in catastrophic incidents and major damages, or unfortunate deaths.

I recall an unfortunate incident when I was employed with a company that manufactured rocket casings. One evening an operator was engaged in the production of a large rocket casing commonly produced by the company. A large rotating devise that assisted in the manufacturing process experienced some binding in the bearings. As a result the bearings overheated. When the operator sensed the overheating condition, he attempted to cool the bearings by applying a wet rag to the bearing housing. The rag he applied happened to be soaked with a highly flammable liquid chemical. The chemical and cloth material combined with the heat from the bearings resulted in a fire. The fire caused enough damage to the rocket casing that resulted in the casing not being suitable for its intended use. Essentially the rocket casing was destroyed. The discarded casing was a $500,000 loss for the company. Fully understand all that you are engaged in so you can avoid making costly mistakes. In this case, the operator knew very little about his operations. Until the incident, the company had only been lucky with this "low knowledge" employee. Failure was simply a matter of time. Are you surrounded with low knowledge individuals on your team or in your company? If so, any success you are enjoying is simply a product of fortune. And failure of your operation is a matter of time. Don't put the potential of success of your relationships in the hands of low knowledge associates. Avoid failure. Understanding what works and why!

I have been privileged in life. I have been afforded the opportunity to work in a variety of employment situations in the Armed Forces, with private companies, and for public sectors organizations. I have worked at every rung of the organizational ladder. I have also had the privilege of operating my own company on several occasions. I have successfully accomplished and achieved at varying levels in academics. I have been allowed to peek behind the scenes of many operations, businesses, teams, relationships, and environments. My observations extend from the nuclear propulsion plant on board the USS Enterprise in the United States Navy to engineering operations at Stanford University to the facility operations at Aerojet and Washington Unified School District in California. I have been privileged and uplifted to observe smart and dedicated people doing amazing work and in control of their circumstance in some very successful companies, programs, and relationships. Because of my vast experience and knowledge, I am often asked whether I've found common denominators in all of these successful situations. I am constantly asked if there is anything one can learn from the common denominators to help turn unfavorable situations into successful ones. The short answer is, yes. Then I say, "Understand whatever you are engaged in to such a degree that no perceived or unexpected circumstance has the power to leave you stranded half-way between where you were and where you want to be. That is the first step."

Spending longer hours in the office to gain critical knowledge of your job and company operations work. Team building exercises to assist everyone in gaining knowledge of how to work better as a team work. Giving leaders the power to replace "low knowledge" and "low performing" employees with "high knowledge" and "high performing" employees works. High expectations work. Giving employees the freedom to grow and develop self-actualization works. Compassionate involvement in the lives of your teammates works. Preparing your professional operations and your personal relationships for unforeseen adversity works. Consistency of effort works. Incentives work. Exposing yourself, and those in your associations, with industry best practices and high standards work.

Indeed, the most important thing I've learned is that none of this is rocket science or some best kept secret. You already know what works, for the most part. The examples are all around us. What most people lack is the true will to do what works. Instead, we have a hotel mentality of expecting convenience over challenges. Our successes tend to existence in the margins of our programs instead of in the great body of our work. Why are our successes the exceptions and not the rule? If we know what works, why don't we simply do it? We frown at spending a few dollars and a few hours a week at the local college increasing our knowledge base, but no one thinks twice about gathering a few hours each day at the local bar during happy hour spending $100 an evening on drinks and appetizers. And $100 goes a long way at a community college. We can not find time to work on our marriages, but we always have time to spend on the phone chatting for hours or time to catch every television show. We can't find time for our children, but we can find time to surf the internet pages of Myspace and Facebook. We fail to pass local bonds to educate our children, even though the system is poorly funding at $5,000 a year per child. Yet we eagerly fund the justice system to lock the uneducated up for life at a cost of $60,000 per year. We know what works to make our lives better, but we fail to act. How does that make sense? I have yet to find a good answer. Instead, I find passivity. Malcolm X said, *"Education is the passport to the future. Tomorrow belongs to those who prepare for it today."* America is starving for truly smart people who understand what works and why. The success and happiness of our lives depend on our ability to bring resolve to this crisis of low knowledge.

THE SIXTH CHALLENGE:

1. Identify knowledge deficiencies in following areas:

 - Your personal relationships

- Your professional relationships

- Your process patterns

- Your Education

- Your Job Training/Professional Skill-set

- Team Building

- Personal Development

2. Identify how you can correct the deficiencies you list.

3. Commit to educating yourself in all areas of your life in which you lack advanced knowledge.

Education does not have to be formal and structured. In fact, the overwhelming quantity of what we learn is not done so in a formal or structured manner. You know what you need to learn. Go learn it! And stop getting stranded half-way to success.

CHALLENGE SEVEN

UNDERSTAND WHAT DOES NOT WORK AND WHY IT DOES NOT WORK

"The relationship between "what is right" and "what is wrong" is so fragile that one wrong act can completely obliterate a lifetime of success. And afterwards, you may have to spend the rest of your life trying to recover what was lost."

—Ronald T. Hickey

Understand what does not work and why. Your life depends on it! Your positive and continuous growth, day after day, month after month, quarter after quarter and year after year; cannot and will not take place until obstacles to developing successful life patterns are eliminated; and knowing what not to do and why is vitally important. Failure to understand what does not work and why it does not work are the very reasons individuals, teams, and organizations waste time, resources, and energy trying to get different results with the same old habits, processes, and traditions. Albert Einstein once stated that, *"The definition of insanity is doing the same thing over and over, but expecting different results."* Then the definition of stupidity must be knowingly doing something that you know does not work over and over, and expecting positive results. Often times, self-stultification, as well as organizational stultification, is the result of not understanding why something does not work, so you keep doing it regardless.

Understanding what does not work and why it does not work is not just simply the opposite of understanding what works and why it works; which was the subject of the previous chapter. Understanding one concept does not necessarily mean you understand the other. The two understandings are partners in success, not opposing competitors. Failure to understand what does not work and why it does not work can be counter productive to success. It is counter productive to success primarily in two functional areas of success. Keep in mind that there are many functional areas of success.

The first functional area adversely affected by not understanding what does not work and why is time. If you expend time engaged in activities that do not work in a particular endeavor, you are wasting valuable time that could be spent engaged in activities that you know will work in the particular endeavor. You can never recover the time, it is forever lost. Additionally, not understanding why an activity does not work exposes you to the risk of repeating the activities over an expanded period of time, further wasting valuable time. Wasting time is counter productive to achieving success because success is often a matter of timing; being in the right place at the right time doing the right things.

The second functional area adversely affected by not understanding why something does not work is progression. Success typically occurs in a progressive manner. We build upon past success to become more successful. Completing tasks that we understand to work in delivering success in a particular endeavor provides for progression toward ultimate achievement. But our progress can be minimized, retarded, or nullified by activities that do no work in the particular endeavor. For example: you can engage in the right activities for 20 years that helps establish someone else's ironclad trust in you. Then one day, you can do just one thing in the relationship that completely wipes away all the trust the person had in you. Because of that one wrong act, you find yourself back at ground zero. All progression has been nullified. Engaging in activities that do not work and not understanding why they do not work is counter productive to success in like manner. One wrong act can erase years of progression toward success. Just think of the time and progression adversely affected in the scandals associated with President Bill Clinton. I am not attempting to cast an inappropriate shadow or light on President Bill Clinton. I personally believe that President Bill Clinton accomplished an enormous amount of great achievements during his time as President of the United States. But he, like everyone, is imperfect. To be human is to be imperfect. But in our imperfections we need to understand just how counter productive and destructive our acts of unrighteousness can be to our lives and the successes we have achieved. President Bill Clinton had to waste a tremendous amount of time dealing with a few of his wrong actions. How much political progression did he erase? This time could have been spent doing things this country needed him to do. Did Bill Clinton's eventual political position in American politics cost Al Gore the Presidency? Who knows? I do know that if any of us fail to understand what does not work in our lives, personal and professional, and why it does not work; we run the risk of losing the equivalent of the time and progression lost by President Bill Clinton in his life, personal and professional. We must consider our wrong acts to a much greater degree than we consider our right acts because our wrong acts have a greater effect on time and progression, as time and progression relates to success.

Don't just simply engage in doing the right things. Doing the right things will only get you so far for so long. You must also commit to "not doing the wrong things." There is a true partnership between doing the right things and not doing the wrong things in life that ultimately defines the level and quality of your success. The quality of the success we experience, more often than not, is defined by just how well we understand what does not work and why it does not work. Most of us do a good job at doing the right things, or at least understanding what the right things to do are. This is not where we fall short. We tend to fall short at "not doing the wrong things" and not understanding why we should not do those wrong things. The failure to "not do wrong things" results in the ultimate failure of the individual, no matter the level of accomplishments achieved. Dennis Kozlowski, the ex-CEO of Tyco International, a company I used to work for, is in prison. He is in prison for the misappropriation of company funds. For what it is worth, Dennis Kozlowski was a good CEO at Tyco, but his failure as a leader was not because of all the good things he did while he was the CEO of Tyco, but because of the wrong things he did. He failed at "not doing the wrong things." The ENRON executives that were convicted and sent to prison failed at "not doing the wrong things." Bernie Madoff, the investment broker who stole approximately 50 billion dollars from investors, failed at "not doing the wrong things", and he will probably end up in prison also. Doing the wrong thing can put you in some very challenging positions and can result in situations that are extremely difficult to recover from. Some even cost you your life or your livelihood.

"Every man is a damn fool for at least five minutes every day; wisdom consists in not exceeding the limit. "

—Elbert Hubbard

I have an older brother who started using drugs in high school. His drug usage continued during his military service right after high school. Robert eventually turned his life over to Christ and became a Minister of the Christian Gospel. He married a wonderful woman and they had three wonderful children together. They both worked hard every day and purchased a home to raise their family. He really turned his life around by understanding what was right and wrong in life and doing those things that made him successful. He and I spoke of the different phases of his life on an occasion. I recall him explaining to me the life of a drug addict. I will never forget it; for the lesson in what he conveyed to me has made a difference in my life and is a basic thesis for this chapter. Robert was addicted to cocaine prior to becoming a Minister. He told me that he had been drug free for over 10 years, but he also said that not a day went by when he did not want to use cocaine. He said the desire and the temptation was as strong 10 years later as it was the first day he stopped. Robert said the desire to use cocaine was constant and unyielding. He said he had to fight this desire with all his might each and every day of his life. He told me that he was constantly aware that his 10 years of being drug free meant nothing if he was unable to get through the current day without using. He said there had even been times when he had gone as far as purchasing the drugs, but later threw them away. The struggle that Robert faces daily with his drug addiction and with doing the right thing and making the right choices is precisely how life works for all of us, whether there is a drug addiction involved or some other addiction. Our years of doing what is right mean absolutely nothing in certain situations, if we are unable to get through the current day without doing wrong. We must always consider what effect one wrong deed will have on the rest of our lives and the lives of those in all of our associations. My brother understood what not to do and why he should not do it. He knew that drugs had the ability to destroy his successful life. He understood drugs would obliterate his progression in life. He understood cocaine would take time away from his life and that he would not be able to recover. He understood. But one day he failed to not use cocaine. He failed at "not doing the wrong thing." Today he is divorced and incarcerated. He has no healthy relationship with any of his three children. Out of incarceration, he is homeless and destitute. A once great man has been decreased. I love my brother dearly and write of him only to offer this valuable lesson to all. The lesson is that all of us have cocaine in our lives as well. Our cocaine may be gambling, infidelity, jealousy, anger, abusiveness, greed, gluttony, drugs, alcohol, or any number of activities that are known to be counter productive to success in life; just ask Dennis Kozlowski, the ENRON executives and Bernie Madoff. It does not matter that you have not used your cocaine in however many years it has been. You must remain vigilant. It is not enough to simply understand. You must partner proper action with that understanding. If you fail and you use your cocaine, you will experience lost time and progression as functions of success; and you will come to know that all of us have a lot more in common with my brother than we care to admit.

If we are going to have successful lives, we must understand what does not work in our lives and why it does not work. We can not be great husbands or wives and cheat on our spouses at the same time. We can not be great parents while we abuse and neglect our children. We can not be great individuals if we fail to understand and not engage in things that do not work in our lives. We can not be great contributors on our teams or in our organizations if our acts are counterproductive to the goals of success. In my marriage I understand that there are many things I can do that are counterproductive to the success of my marriage. I quickly realized that the manner in which I speak to my wife determines the quality of the relationship on any and every given day. In my understanding of my own marital relationship and human relationships in general, I have learned that there are at least five occasions each day that a person speaks and those spoken words work against success or are counterproductive to progress in their relationships. If a person can learn what those five things are and eliminate them from their daily vocabulary, a person can have a more successful day. In an attempt to be a great husband, I realized that there are things I could say to my wife that are in no way beneficial to our relationship. Words can be very damaging if uttered in an irresponsible manner. I focus on not speaking to my wife in an inappropriate manner. I realize that one wrongly spoken word can cause the two of us not to speak to one another for days. If we go days without speaking because of harmful words I have spoken, then that is time we lose as husband and wife and it impedes our progression to peace, love, harmony, and happiness with one another. Likewise, if I generate a hostile work environment at my job or a tension filled atmosphere within one of my social associations, I cause a loss of time and progression within those relationships. Much good can be destroyed with something as small as the human tongue. Understand what not to say in all of your relationships and why. If you can eliminate the five occasions each day in which you verbally utter counterproductively, you will be successful in providing an atmosphere more congenial for the pursuit of happiness in your personal life and greatness in your professional life.

To assist in managing the words I speak to and/or about another person, I utilize a test that a great friend of mine introduced me to. My friend referred to it as the Socrates Triple Filter Test. I made some changes to the test because in the Socrates Triple Filter Test your intended statement need only pass one of the three tests. In my test, the intended statement must pass all three tests. I refer to this test as the Positive Statement Filter Test. If your statements are always "beneficial fact-based positive words" then your statements should always forward your positive agenda. Essentially, success is promoted by your words when your words are factual, positive, and beneficial. The Positive Statement Filter Test consists of filtering your words through three questions as filters.

POSITIVE STATEMENT FILTER TEST:

The first filter is the **FACT FILTER**. Ask yourself, "Is the statement factual?" If your answer is no, resist making the statement. Your family, friends, co-workers, acquaintances, and associates should be able to trust your every word. If you speak it, it ought to be as good as gold. One is hard pressed to find anything more counterproductive to success and/or damaging to a person's reputation than being labeled or thought of as a liar or someone who does not verify his or her information. If you are not sure of your facts, research the information until you are sure. If the statement is unequivocally factual, then proceed to the next filter before you offer the statement to anyone.

The second filter is the **POSITIVE FILTER**. Ask yourself, "Is the statement a positive statement?" If the statement is positive it should have no negative effects whatsoever. Simply because a statement is factual does not suggest the statement is positive. Gossip, for example, is comprised primarily of factual information about someone; but is normally negative in nature. A positive statement should be a statement that any reasonable person would welcome. Another manner in which to determine if a statement is positive is to ask yourself if you would make the statement if the person who is the subject or object of your statement was standing next to you. Remember, words are like boomerangs; everything you say comes back to you. If the statement is not a positive statement, resist making the statement. No one really likes a gossiper, and no one really trusts a person unwilling to stand in front of his or her words. As the saying goes, "Loose lips sink ships." Loose lips can also derail your train to success. How often have you shared your dreams or ideas with someone, only to have him or her say something negative to deter you from pursuing those dreams or ideas? Words are powerful, whether negative or positive. Now, if the statement is a positive statement, proceed to the final filter before making the statement.

The third and final filter is the **BENEFIT FILTER**. Ask yourself, "Is the statement beneficial to anyone?" Your statements should be something that someone deems as useful in his or her efforts to build upon success, happiness, harmony, trust, or something good and desirable in his or her life. When you are a benefit to someone, either in word or deed, you are a tremendous and invaluable asset to that person's success. In turn, that person becomes a tremendous and invaluable asset to your success. So, if your statements are factual, positive, and beneficial, utter them freely and often. Your success and the success of those around you depend on your positive statements.

Deploying the English language inappropriately is another example of how we unnecessarily fail at "not doing the wrong thing." I say unnecessarily, because everyone can learn to be more disciplined in our language utilization. The Positive Statement Filter Test works for me. There may be another process that works for you. But whatever works, be disciplined in using what works. Words are very powerful. If loose lips sink ships, then disciplined words steer the course. The following story will convey how failing to filter your words steer your relationships off course and into troubled waters. My wife and I were having dinner one evening with friends at their home. The wife of the couple had worked hard at preparing dinner. In the middle of dinner, the wife turned to her husband and asked his opinion on how one of the dishes turned out. The husband made some very negative statements about the dish. He said the dish was the worse he had tasted and wondered what she had done to make it taste so bad. Of course the conversation at the table became strained after his statements. Everyone knows that you do not speak negatively about the food in the middle of dinner. No woman, and no man for that matter, wants to hear that the food is horrible; especially in front of guests while everyone is seated at the dinner table. The next day, my friend called to inform me that he and his wife had a heated argument after dinner concerning the inappropriate nature of his comments about the food she had prepared. He stated that he and his wife were currently not speaking to one another as a result of the argument. He asked if I thought his statement was wrong or inappropriate. I replied with a resounding, "Yes!" He asked why I felt he was wrong or why the statement was inappropriate if the statement was his honest answer. I told him that his statement did not pass the Positive Statement Filter Test. While in his opinion the statement was factual, the statement was not positive and was not of benefit to anyone. You should never be willing to make a statement based solely on position that the statement is factual; not if your intent is to maintain harmony in your relationship(s).

Utilizing the Positive Statement Filter Test is very useful in the work place as well. In fact, it may be even more useful in the work place because words are truly like boomerangs in our places of employment. Everything you say on the job, especially the negative, no matter what your position is in your organization, will definitely come back to you. In every organization I have worked, there had always been situations that involved negative talk. This negative talk, even if factual information was included, resulted in a less than desirable atmosphere. Negative talk produces tension, jealousy, strife, dissention, and a variety of other cantankerous work environments. Whatever the exact atmosphere produced by this failure to not understand what does not work and why, the atmosphere is counterproductive to every goal of the organization. Because of the atmosphere produced by negative talk, success, if achieved at all, requires increased efforts on everyone's part. When employees fail to understand that negative talk does not work in the work place, organizational goals become much more challenging; team efforts become less effective; and the workforce becomes disenfranchised. I have worked in such places, and I have been part of such teams. Everyone is there just for the paycheck or for some false expectation. Eventually, the organization and/or team experience its demise. Companies and organizations lose great employees and team players because of the atmosphere generated by negative talk. I know many organizations extend a significant amount of resources in training personnel. A very minimum amount, if any, of those resources are deployed to train people on exactly how to avoid the five statements they make each day at work that are counterproductive to the organization's goals. Many of us recall the unfortunate circumstances that resulted in NBA All-Star guard/forward Latrell Sprewell physically attacking his coach, P.J. Carlesimo on December 1, 1997; when both were with the Golden State Warriors NBA franchise. Latrell Sprewell was a 4 time NBA All-Star. His career averages are 18.8 points per game, 4.2 assists per game, and 4.1 rebounds per game. But he is mostly remembered for the events of December 1, 1997. The situation leading up to the choking incident resulted from statements both men made to one another over time. An otherwise remarkable professional basketball career is forever overshadowed by one avoidable event that was made possible in an atmosphere created by negative talk. One wrong act can nullify a career of great accomplishments and take the rest of your life to overcome. Latrell Sprewell had his contract cancelled with the Golden State Warriors. The remaining contract was worth $25 million. Understand what does not work and why.

Now, if there are at least five occasions each day in which we speak counterproductively, there are surely occasions each day in which we act counterproductively. If those actions can be identified, then they can be eliminated. I am sure Latrell Sprewell would welcome the opportunity to take back choking P.J. Carlesimo. Luckily I have never had to deal with managing the efforts of millionaire athletes. But I have been in many situations in which I supervised the output of adults in the American workforce. The American worker will make a living out of being counterproductive if allowed to do so. I have been graced to have managed personnel the majority of my life in a variety of sectors. Fortunately, most of those I have managed have been disciplined employees. But I have had my share of unproductive employees to deal with. Because of my engineering background, more often than not, I have supervised and managed skilled craft technicians of the building, industrial, manufacturing, and engineering trades. Within these fields, there has always been a need to increase productivity. This increase in productivity is referred to as increasing "tool time." So "more tool time" meant the employee was spending more time engaged in actual productive work that could be measured at the end of the work day. So, in an effort to always increase "tool time", I always evaluated the daily activities of the employees to identify activities that were counterproductive to "tool time." Once I identify those counterproductive activities, I would then simply figure out a way to eliminate those activities from the employees' daily routine. For instance, at one place of employment, the landscapers reported to work at 6:00 AM, but did not actually start any productive work until approximately 7:00 AM. That was an automatic loss of one hour of "tool time" each day. When asked why they did not commence any productive work until 7:00 AM, the groundskeepers informed me that the excuse was because there was not enough day light available for them to see what they were doing until approximately 7:00 AM. As a result, I changed their start time to 7:00 AM. Starting work at 6:00 AM was not working because there remained darkness at 6:00 AM. Understanding what was not working and why provided the answer to the problem. As simple as this may seem, many activities in our lives go unchanged because this simple process is never employed in our lives. If you don't have enough "tool time" in you life activities, evaluate your daily activities and identify where you are wasting time. Understand what is not working in your life and why. Many of us are not successful because the daily activities of our lives are filled with wasting time counterproductively. If we can eliminate the waste in our lives, we can generate the opportunity to engage our time with more productive activities. If we understand what does not work and why it does not work, then we can avoid worthless efforts and provide for more time to engage in activities proven to produce success. How much time do you waste each day to counterproductive activities that are holding you at bay from the success you say you want?

Understand that activities counterproductive to achieving your goals defer and prevent your success. Counterproductiveness does not work! Negative words and negative deeds work against you. Don't work against yourself. Determine your desired destiny in life and let your every effort be effective in progressing you toward that end. Do not carry past errors in your life forward. Correct your errors immediately so you don't waste time and energy repeating your actions. Success is progressive and time sensitive. When you fail to understand what does not work and why; you run the risk of having many false starts, start-over's, re-do's, and lost time. Act as if your spouse, boss, coach, mother, father, children, spiritual leader, and associates are always watching and listening. Resist that extremely strong propensity to do wrong. Doing wrong can cost you your life and erase all of your accomplishments. Don't climb to the top of the ladder just to jump off. Don't climb the ladder to CEO just to go to jail for a wrong doing. Don't work hard at being the next NBA All-Star just so you can later throw away a multi-million dollar contract. And remember, yesterday's success means very little if you throw it all away today. Understand what does not work and why.

To emphasize this point, allow me to tell you a story about a poor old peasant that lived in a barn out in the countryside. There was once an old peasant that worked the fields for a very rich aristocrat. The peasant figured that the rich aristocrat had more than the aristocrat would ever need. So he decided that each day he would take a little grain from the harvest he was employed to take in. He figured the rich aristocrat would never miss the grain if he took a little each day. The peasant's plan was to save up enough grain to eventually go into business for himself and get rich. One morning he awoke and noticed the rats had torn into his grain sack and eaten a good portion of the grain he was taking for himself. The peasant decided to tie the sack of grain to a rafter in the barn in which he slept. He believed that allowing the sack of grain to hang from the ceiling rafters so the rats could not get to it was a great means of keeping the grain safe. The peasant also decided to sleep under the sack of grain for added security. One night, a wise old rat climbed atop the rafter and ate through the rope that tied the sack to the rafters. The heavy sack of grain fell and landed directly on the head of the peasant, killing him instantly.

POSITIVE ACTION FILTER TEST:

You must learn to triple filter your actions as well. Filtering your actions are as important as filtering your words. The following is a discussion on filtering your actions:

The first filter is the **HONESTY FILTER**. Are your actions honest? God will not bless dishonesty. You may get away with dishonesty for a while, but all bad deeds eventually catch up with you. And the punishment will be unbearably harsh. Dishonesty does not produce any form of success. Many people engaged in illegal activity may be thought of as successful. Trust me, their only success will ultimately be ruining their lives and the lives of those around them. Honesty is the first character a successful person must possess. Without honesty, nothing you ever accomplish will ever really mean much to anyone but you. And success is a very lonely place if you are the only one there.

The second filter is the **GOODNESS FILTER**. Are your actions for the sake of goodness? Your actions should have a planned positive effect on someone's life or some organization's goal. Put forth your best effort in your actions so that you provide the greatest good in all that you do. You take big steps down the path to success when you produce great acts of goodness. Goodness is having your heart in the right place. And your heart must be seriously involved for success to manifest from your deeds. Your heart determines the level of your commitment. Your level of commitment creates the manner of your goodness. A committed heart is the second character a successful person must possess.

The third and final filter is the **EFFECTIVE FILTER**. Are your actions effective in progressing your efforts toward your desired destiny? Highly successful people have an uncanny ability to focus their efforts like a laser beam onto their desired achievements. This focused effort produces success in a very efficient manner. When you eat, drink, think, and dream success; all of your efforts will be focused on your goals; and you will come to know success. You will refuse to be denied. The third character a successful person must possess is the desire to want something enough to sacrifice his or her wants for what he or she needs.

THE SEVENTH CHALLENGE:

1. List everything that is not working in your life. Write down why those things do not work in your life. Determine how you can eliminate these things from your life.

2. Complete item #1 for your job and all the teams you are associated with. Approach this item from a professional perspective. What is not working in your professional associations?

3. Determine the five occasions each day in which

you speak inappropriately to someone in your family. Use the Positive Statement Filter Test by determining if your intended statements are factual, positive, and beneficial.

4. Complete item #3 for your job and all the teams you are associated with.

5. Evaluate your daily activities. Identify all counterproductive activities. Eliminate all counterproductive activities from your daily routine.

6. List your negative addictions. Identify the addictions that have the ability to completely destroy your life. Commit to obtaining professional help with your addictions.

7. Triple filter your actions. Ask yourself if your actions are honest, good, and effective.

8. Triple filter your words. Ask yourself if your words are factual, positive and a benefit to someone.

Challenge Eight

Trust In Your Own Abilities

"There is absolutely no possibility for success and happiness in your life without first trusting in your own abilities. Because believe it or not; you are always right about yourself. If you say you can, you can. If you say you can't, you can't."

—Ronald T. Hickey

The reason so many of us fail to experience our full potential is because we don't believe in ourselves. We don't truly believe we have the talents and abilities to achieve the things we say we want to achieve. We tell ourselves that we can't. And if you say you can't, you can't. Often times our own disbelief in our capacity to accomplish a task prevents us from being successful. While someone outside and beyond us may plant the idea in our minds that we can not succeed at something, our own willingness to accept and believe the same is the true reason many of us continue to live a life of mediocrity. Simply stated, your own inability to trust in yourself, your abilities, your talents, and your knowledge, is precisely why you experience low achievement in your life. Each of us can significantly change our conditions for the better simply by believing we can do the things we say we want to do and expect success. Decide today that your life is going to be everything you wish your life to be, and believe with all your heart and soul that you have all the abilities necessary to bring your desired life into full fruition. Know that if you say you can, you can. So, at this moment, on this day, say, "I can!" If you don't know it, learn it. If you don't have it, get it. From this day forth, make your actions count and do not falter in your determination to fulfill your destiny. Believe with all that you are that God has given you all that you need to become the greatest You. Believe in yourself and the abilities bestowed upon you. Refuse, wholeheartedly, to follow the destiny outlined in some mystical imaginative world. Understand what you are capable of; commit to staying in your lane, and create your own unique life. Trust in your own abilities and be the best You!

I believe your resolve to leave deep footprints in the path of life is your best asset. Without such drive and motivation, you limit the value of the journey. While the end is unavoidable, let it not be from loss of will or lack of resolve, but because you have nothing left to give and your time has come. You have the ability to do something on a grand scale, each of us do. Learn what that something is and understand that your life has been a process in which you have collected all that is necessary for you to do that something better than anyone. Do not give up your resolve to imprint upon this earth your true gifts. When others say you can do no more, keep moving. As long as you can keep going, use your imagination to cope with the travails of life. You are never burdened beyond what you can carry, no matter how heavy the burden may seem at times. The weight of the universe is not meant to break you, but to shape you.

Overcome your obstacles and realize what you envision. If you lack the education to move up in your organization, go back to school and gain the necessary education. If you know you don't have the funds to open up a business you have always dreamed of owning and operating, get a second job or third job to save the money. If something is standing in the way of your achievement; trust in your abilities to go around, under, over, or through the obstacle. If your spouse, friend, co-worker, or anyone is telling you that you can not do something and you know that you can; don't listen. Do what you know you are here to do.

I recall years ago while serving in the United States Navy when I sat across the table from an educational and career counselor who told me I would not make it through the Naval Nuclear Power School in Orlando, Florida. I had just completed an electrical training course at the Naval Training Center in Great Lakes, Illinois and was scheduled to commence Nuclear Power and Nuclear Theory training. At the time when I was enrolled in Naval Nuclear Power School, the school was ranked #2, only to MIT. This was based upon the attrition rate of student enrollment. I understood that the school would be my greatest academic challenge, but I knew and trusted my abilities. This counselor's knowledge of me was very limited. All he knew of me was contained in the academic report sitting in front of him. That academic report only conveyed that I was a highly intelligent person with no known academic limits. I rejected the words of the counselor and graduated from the school. A few years later, while stationed on board the aircraft carrier the U.S.S. Enterprise, I was in charge of all electrical plant operations for two nuclear reactor plants. One year afterwards, I was resonsible for all reactr plant electrical systems training for a 500 personnel Reactor Department. But the counselor told me I was not going to make it through the school. I had the final say in this matter. I trusted in my knowledge, talents, and academic abilities. I said I could, and I did.

In no way am I suggesting that you will not know unexpected sadness, failure, and defeat. Life is not perfect, and things do not always work out the way you wish. You will experience failure on occasion. You will meet with defeat from time to time. You will know the sorrow of seeing what is dearest to you taken from you right before your eyes. Life is very challenging at times, and no one wins every single time. Accept that fact, but do not allow set backs to cause you to doubt yourself. The nature of human existence ensures that you will experience the bitterness of life, but the power of trusting in your own abilities will guarantee that such sourness is short lived. Know that you will fall in life, but trust you will always have the ability to get back up on your feet. Know that you will come up short in the race on one day, but capture the gold medal the next day. Life is a dualistic existence, in the sense that everything you experience has an opposite. There is sunshine and rain. There is good and bad. There are mountain tops and there are valleys. You fail and succeed in life. You rise and fall. You live and die. What you do in between the opposites of your circumstance determines the heights of your travel and the quality of your life. You will experince both joy and pain, both success and failure, and both negative and positive. The worst thing you can do is get down on yourself and start wasting precious time buffering the facts of life with fairytales and illogical explanations. I have learned that failures, defeats, set-backs, and sorrow all have built in lessons that ultimately provide me with invaluable knowledge and understanding that will be necessary in the near future for me to be successful. Going through certain situations is the only way of gaining a particular knowledge at times. God makes us suffer defeat today so we can be triumphant tomorrow. Through the suffering, we must believe and trust we are going to be better on the other end. Imagine the suffering that Tony Dungy and his family were required to endure with the loss of his oldest child. Tony Dungy emerged from that situation believing and trusting more in God, his family, his team, and his abilities. As a result, the following year he was the first African-American head football coach in the NFL to lead his team to a Super Bowl Championship.

As I stated earlier, you are capable of carrying your cross, even though you may not think so at the time of burden. If you lose or have lost your job, trust that your abilities will ensure you will find a better job. If your marriage is in trouble, trust that you have the knowledge to right all the wrongs and make your relationship stronger. Adversity aids the temper process of life. Just as steel is subjected to extreme heat and cold temperatures in the tempering process to make the steel almost unbreakable, adversity is the heat that tempers your life and makes you strong and durable. Remain keenly aware that each day, your life grows shorter by twenty-four hours. The time and energy available to achieve success and grandiosity becomes more precious. The tempering in life is necessary for you to obtain such levels of sustainable achievements. Tempering is not intended to weaken you; but rather strengthen you with unyielding confidence and wisdom that your natural talents and developed abilities will deliver the life you desire, if only you trust in yourself. With such trust, you must fulfill everything you want in life. Your life is a creation that evolves as you desire and believe. Trust that you can, and you will. Give up your doubtful notions; and in so doing, you will finally emerge completely with your destiny. Until that moment, create the successful pathways of your life with confidence, passion, purpose and determination.

"I've spent most of my life walking under that hovering cloud, self-doubt, whose acid raindrops blurred my vision and burned holes in my heart. Once I learned to use the umbrella of confidence, the skies cleared up for me and the sunshine called joy became my faithful companion."

—Astrid Alauda

After my military career came to an end in 1992, I went to work for a global industrial metals company. I was hired as a journeyman electrician in one of the company's many industrial manufacturing plants. This particular plant was located in the California Bay Area. After about six months on the job, my supervisor resigned for a better opportunity with another company. The plant was in the middle of an expansion project to provide an increase in production capacity. Part of the expansion project included 150 yards of additional conveyance controlled by a programmable limit controller (PLC) that digitally operated sensors, motors, and other electrical peripherals by way of a software program referred to as ladder logic. The entire project had been designed by engineers at the company's headquarters back East. My supervisor, who had just resigned, was the one who normally did all the programming, writing the ladder logic software program, of the programmable limit controllers in the plant. PLC's were a new industry device in the early 1990's, and I knew very little about them since the Navy, where I had worked the past 8 years, had not advanced to the new digital technology. The Navy was still using electro-mechanical systems which included pushbuttons, electrical switches, mechanical valves, and etc. to operate electrical systems. PLC's used a technology that allowed operating electrical and mechanical systems with digital software, instead of human interactions to push buttons to start electrical motors. Eventhough I had not been at the plant in the Bay Area for long, I knew the basics and learned all I could about PLC's every opportunity I had. While I had only been employed by the company for six months, I knew more about the new technology than the other electricians who had been working at the plant for years. The other electricians expressed no interest in learning the new PLC technology. So, when my supervisor walked out the door, the big expansion project was put on hold. No one at the plant could program the PLC's, and headquarters was not committed to sending an engineer to the Bay Area. So, all the thousands of dollars invested in new equipment was at risk.

I knew I understood the basics of writing ladder logic, and I also knew that I had the ability to review the engineering designs for the expansion project to determine how the system was designed to operate. So, I took the initiative to take a few manuals home. I learned, to the advanced level, about programmable limit controllers and writing ladder logic for PLC programs. After two weeks of reading all of the manuals, I started spending my lunch and work breaks working to finish the expansion project. I tested all the electrical motors, sensors, electronic counters, interlocks, and all other electrical and mechanical devices for proper operations. No one at the plant was aware of what I was doing on my own time. I began to develop the ladder logic for the PLC to operate the 150 yards of conveyance. I wrote the ladder logic to operate the system based on how the engineering designs suggested everything should work. I recall the night I was working and loaded the ladder logic into the main PLC module for the first time during my lunch break. From the laptop computer, I initiated a "run" signal for the program to operate the large conveyance system, and like magic, everything operated as should. I had the biggest grin across my face. I had to make some minor adjustments in the ladder logic and adjust positions of some sensors associated with the conveyor system, but everything worked. I was so focused that I had not realized that I had an audience. Everyone on the night shift in the manufacturing plant was curious about all the new equipment that was now operating. After an hour or so, the plant manager showed up at the plant. The night shift production supervisor had called him to report what was going on. The plant manager demanded that I demonstrate all that I had done. Once he was absolutely sure everything was operating as required, he finally shook my hand, had a bigger grin on his face than was on mine, and ordered me to meet him in his office the next morning at 10:00 AM. When I arrived for the meeting, he offered me the plant electrical supervisor's position. I trusted my abilities and was confident that I could learn what I needed to know to make that project a success. In less than seven months on the job, I was promoted over employees who worked in the plant for more than 25 years. That was the ultimate pay-off for me trusting in my own natural talents and developed abilities.

Trusting in your own ability is intended to lead to self-sufficiency. No one else assisted me in the conveyance project. As a result of my self-sufficiency, the plant I worked for did not have to rely on headquarters for engineering services, so the plant became self-sufficient as a result. Whatever one needs to do in life, one should be able to do on one's own. Being able to help yourself does not mean you will always have or know what you need at any given moment.

Just like in the conveyance example above, sometimes you have to delay moving forward until you have taken the time to understand your limits and have gone out and gained the knowledge necessary to satisfy the challenges associated with the situations you find yourself in. But you must trust you have the ability to do such. Whether you are dealing with conflict at work or working on a challenging project at home, you should be able to cope with aplomb and ease.

Mike Tomlin became the second African-American to lead a National Football League franchise to a Super Bowl Championship on February 1, 2009. He accomplished this outstanding feat at the age of 36 and during his second season as the head coach of the Pittsburg Steelers. When asked by a sports reporter referencing his youthfulness and short tenure as head coach if he had doubted his ability and questioned his experience to lead the franchise to their NFL record setting sixth Super Bowl championship, Mike Tomlin replied with conviction that he never doubted his abilities. He affirmed that the Rooney family, the owners of the Pittsburg Steelers, knew the business of football. Mike Tomlin stated that if the Rooney's had the confidence to give him the job, then he knew he had all the necessary tools for being successful. Mike Tomlin told himself that he could win a Super Bowl Championship as the head coach of the Pittsburg Steelers, and he did just that in only two years. Trusting yourself is paramount to being successful.

"To be successful you have to be selfish, or else you never achieve. And once you get to your highest level, then you have to be unselfish. Stay reachable. Stay in touch. Don't isolate."

—Michael Jordan

Success has a tendency to make you feel isolated at the top. The degree of isolation depends on just how far success has removed you from the masses. While being very successful comes with a great deal of self-sufficiency, being self-sufficient is not the same as being isolated. The country of China provides a good example of isolation. When the king of China closed the China borders years ago, the country was self-sufficient enough to enjoy their isolation. The entire nation withdrew into a magical contentment. They felt that the country was better off without the meddling outside influences from other countries. But eventually an inbred society developed. Stagnation and decay set in. An identical issue can arise in people who believe they are so self-sufficient that they fail to engage life fully. Either they will implode from the sheer weight of their own decadence and stagnation, or they will explode from being isolated with only their own thoughts. Just as China began to flourish and experience the greatness of life once they re-opened their borders to the outside world, humans must remain open to outside influences, stimuli, and information if we are to experience the possibilities of greatness. Life can not be lived in a vacuum, at least not a very good life. The grandiosity of life can not be realized by only wandering about the margins of this human episode. The abundance of life is nebulous in nature, and every situation, condition, and time has the potential for providing explosive joy. Expect success as you traverse the abyss of time as you follow the intuitions of your heart and take each step with the confidence that you are where you are as a result of God's grace and the abilities He has bestowed upon you. Step out of the margins and onto the full pages of life with intrepidness and determination. Trust in you! Those who trust in their own abilities and are self-sufficient roam the world and succeed without bounds. The self-sufficient may avail themselves to the opportunistic, occasional, and temporary advantage of withdrawal and intense self-cultivation and self-preservation, but they do not become permanently isolated. People gifted with self-sufficiency and self-confidence are constantly forging forward in all circumstances with their knowledge illuminating the path. They are excitedly in constant motion, attracting vast knowledge, engaged by favorable happenstance; and therefore, avoid decadence and staleness.

"Every day we slaughter our finest impulses. That is why we get a heart-ache when we read those lines written by the hand of a master and recognize them as our own, as the tender shoots which we stifled because we lacked the faith to believe in our own powers, our own criterion of truth and beauty. Every man, when he gets quiet, when he becomes desperately honest with himself, is capable of uttering profound truths. We all derive from the same source. There is no mystery about the origin of things. We are all part of creation, all kings, all poets, all musicians; we have only to open up, to discover what is already there."

—Henry Miller, *Sexus*

You may be capable of great things, but you have to open up and discover what is already within you. You may only see little things when you look at yourself. You may be of meager beginnings. You may not have graduated Summa Cum Laude from an Ivy League school. You may still be in an entry level position. You may not be exactly where you want to be. Do not suppress those little things because life consists overwhelmingly of small things. Big things seldom come along. You should embrace the small things about you as well as the big things. The big and the small have made you who you are. Big things do not occur until a lot of little things have come together on behalf of some great accomplishment. A big book is but an orderly collection of a volume of small words combined in such a manner that they convey a literary context. Your big life is but a summation of all the small daily things you have accomplished. Remember, you crawled before you walked. You mumbled small words before you uttered a complete sentence. The small things we complete give rise to our beliefs that we are capable of something larger. We may all desire vehemently to make grand and lasting achievements, to invent a new process or product that makes our company billions of dollars, or to be the one who saves the damsel in distress, but life seldom affords us the opportunities to make billions, become heroes, or accomplish great achievements. But we all have the ability to be great at the small things that dominate our lives. We can be great at the small daily tasks that make us great spouses and great parents. We can be great at small daily activities and interactions that make us great co-workers and contributors on the job. We can be great at listening to our friends, fishing with our grandfather, shopping with our mother, or cooking with our family. The grandiosity of life emerges from our unwavering ability to excel at these small things. If a child does not master the science of math or the art of English, he or she can not become a great scientist or orator one day. If you want to be successful, give much attention to mastering the small things. If you don't master the small steps in life, you will not develop trust in your abilities to conquer the mountain. I will again use Michael Jordan's NBA career to emphasize a point. Michael will be mentioned in the following chapter as well. Michael Jordan, one of the world's greatest sports champions, missed more than 9,000 shots in his basketball career. He missed the game winning shot 26 times. He also won six NBA Championships because he and his teammates believed he had the ability to make every shot he attempted. Despite missing the game winning shot 26 times, his coaches and teammates believed he had the ability to make the winning shots. Michael Jordan was great at the small things. He mastered the mundane daily steps of his trade. Michael was the consummate competitor and trusted in his abilities, despite his numerous misses. As a result, he gave himself and the Chicago Bulls franchise the opportunity to win championships. He conquered the mountain six times. When you trust in your natural and developed ability to master the small steps of your life, you provide yourself future opportunities to accomplish great achievements.

"Mediocrity is walking a tightrope and holding onto a handrail. Excellence is when you no longer need the handrail. Grandiosity is when you are the handrail. You are the handrail when others lean on you to balance themselves as they walk the tightrope of life."

—Ronald T. Hickey

Some years ago I owned a condominium unit in a large commercial complex. My unit was on the eleventh floor. One evening a friend and I had returned from dining out to find the electrical power to the entire complex had been lost. The entire facility was pitch-dark. I told my friend we would have to walk the entire eleven flights to get to my unit. She did not think that was such a good idea because she understood we would not be able to see where we were going. I told her not to be concerned because I could safely and securely find our way. She trusted me and took my hand. We entered the building from a street level entry door and maneuvered our way to the eleventh floor and directly to the door that accessed my unit. Once inside, I lit candles and we adjusted our faculties. My friend expressed how impressed she was that I was able to find my way in complete darkness without making any wrong turns, or causing injury to her or myself. I told her that while I served on board the USS Enterprise, an aircraft carrier in the Navy, we had to learn how to travel safely to and from various locations within the ship in similar conditions. In the Navy I was required, via scheduled emergency drill exercises, to practice and demonstrate my ability to move through the large aircraft carrier safely and securely. On an U.S. Navy "made for war ship", there were a variety of situations that would warrant everyone on board having the ability to travel about the ship in complete darkness. Your life could depend on your ability to get topside from ten levels below deck from a variety of locations during such emergencies as a compartment fire, engineering plant flood, or accident in the weapons magazine. I felt this was such good training that it could save my life or someone else's life one day even as a civilian. So everywhere I lived, I trained myself to be able to travel in complete darkness throughout the building in case of any sort of emergency that required evacuation. The condominium complex was no exception. I had practiced on many occasions. So when the night came to utilize my training, I was confident in my ability to safely and securely find our way to my unit in total darkness. To this day, I continue to practice this technique. I realized after years of practice that there is a great lesson in always striving to be prepared for the unknown. The lesson is life is often uncertain. Things happen that are simply beyond your control. During such times of uncertainty and challenge, you may sense you are blindly navigating with an urgency to survive safely and securely. You may be experiencing problems with your spouse or children. You may have a parent with failing health. You may be in a situation where you are suddenly asked to assume a role of greater responsibility at work, or you may have a new supervisor that is not sensitive to your needs as a professional. How well you have trained and prepared yourself to deal with life's many anomalies will ultimately establish the degree to which you trust your own abilities to see yourself through. Exactly to what degree you trust in your training, preparedness, and abilities will determine the efficacy of your efforts to move from point A to B with no detriment to your overall well-being. Circumstances may dictate that you find other employment. Situations could force the demise of relationships. The current depressive global economy of 2009 has the undoubted potential of bringing a plethora of unforeseeable and unfortunate events into fruition in your life. Understand that the necessary and unpleasant walk in the dark will require you to summons all that you are, your abilities, and confidence in a concerted effort to secure your safe travel. Who you are, your abilities, and your trust of these abilities will be the milieu that decides your fate. Essentially, your abilities and the degree to which you trust your abilities are what make or break you in every situation in life. You can not always control the stimuli, but you control the response unequivocally. The outcome is normally what you expect, or at least what you should expect.

"Expectations are derived from your belief that you have the abilities to succeed at something. The greater you think of your abilities, the higher your expectations will be. You succeed when you expect to do so. You expect to do so when you believe you have the ability."

—Ronald T. Hickey

If you can not trust your own abilities, or the abilities of your teammates, to critically think to bring resolve to fundamental problems in your process patterns, you will never reach your full potential and your team will never experience the success that only comes from interdependency. Whether you consider your team to be your family, a group of co-workers, or social acquaintances; your success depends on the self-sufficiency that only results from complete trust in one another's abilities. There are only a few things that are more counterproductive to success within a teamwork atmosphere than a person who does not trust his or her teammates. I repeat the following question from a previous chapter because it is worth repeating here: Have you ever noticed the difference in NBA Superstars Allen Iverson, Kobe Bryant or Paul Pierce when they play with teammates they trust, as opposed to teammates they do not trust? Remember, as stated previously, just like with these NBA Superstars, if you trust your teammates, your individual statistics will decrease, but the team's success rate increases. And vice versa, if you do not trust your teammates, your statistics increase, but the team's success rate decreases. I would say, beyond a shadow of a doubt, that trusting in your abilities and the abilities of your teammates are synonymous with a high success rate of any team in any organization.

About Your Abilities...you should have the capacity to:

- Create opportunities for yourself,
- Bring resolve to fundamental problems you face,
- Create trust between you and others,
- Overcome any obstacle that exists in your pathways,
- Remain progressive during times of extreme challenge,
- Develop self-sufficiency without promoting isolation, and

THE EIGHTH CHALLENGE:

Ask yourself the following:

1. Am I self-sufficient? If not, determine what you need to do to become so.

2. Am I the handrail or holding on to it?

3. Can I navigate life during times of challenges?

4. Do I have enough education?

5. Do I have enough knowledge?

6. Do I have enough skill?

7. Am I on the right team?

8. Do I trust the abilities of my teammates?

9. Do my teammates trust my abilities?

10. Can I create the opportunities for success?

Do the following:

1. Never again utter the words, "I Can't."

2. If you can not say with absolute confidence, "I Can!" Then;

    a. Learn it, or

    b. Get it, or

    c. Create it, or

    d. Change it.

CHALLENGE NINE

LEARN FROM YOUR EXPERIENCES

"A man who carries a cat by the tail learns something he can learn in no other way."

—Mark Twain

"I've missed more than 9000 shots in my career. I've lost almost 300 games. 26 times, I've been trusted to take the game winning shot and missed. I've failed over and over and over again in my life. And that is why I succeed."

—Michael Jordan

Experience allows learning from both mistakes and successes. Mastering the art of learning from experience requires one to constantly ask, "What did I do wrong?" and "What did I do right?" This continual examination process where you execute and then evaluate your actions is the delineation that depicts your areas of success and your areas of needed improvements. The idea is to move away from seeing anything as a mistake, but rather as an experience to learn from. As you learn from each experience the contours of success should increase steadily over time. If your failure profile is consistently larger than your success profile, you are not learning from your mistakes, and you will find yourself in the perpetual motion of repeating mishaps. Learning from your experiences is paramount for developing trust in your abilities and the abilities of those in your associations. Michael Jordan stated that he missed more than 9,000 shots in his career. He must have evaluated every missed shot and learned something as a result because no one remembers any of the 9,000 shots he missed. We remember all those big shots he did make. That's what learning from your mistakes does for you. It puts you in the position to successfully make the big shots. If you can not examine and grade your own work, then it becomes essentially impossible to establish the degree of your abilities in reference to the full potential germane to the process. You simply must learn from your experiences, successes and failures, if you wish to become highly successful and make grand achievements.

"Few people even scratch the surface; much less exhaust the contemplations of their own experiences."

—Randolph Bourne

While missteps, mishaps, false starts, errors, and misjudgments all present tremendous learning opportunities, you can only learn from a given situation if you realize you have come up short in obtaining your goal. Thus, awareness is the first step in the process of learning from your experiences. If you are not aware that your actions are incorrect, then you will not seek to alter them. This lack of knowledge keeps you at bay from any potential lesson. But if you understand the importance of constantly asking yourself if your actions are correct, then you will maintain a vigilant approach to the learning process. Identification of a mistake, even if only briefly outlined, provides for the learning possibilities by allowing you to concentrate your efforts for greater understanding. Wise people are adamant about examining all their efforts to ensure they are always deploying the best approach to enhance the possibility of optimum success. Highly successful people accept the fact that progress toward their goals is supported only by such constant evaluations of their actions.

Realizing and understanding mistakes and failures afford us the opportunity to become better in all that we do. Mistakes and failures often times provide us our greatest lessons in life. Additionally, many lessons can only be learned by means of committing a mistake or failing miserably at something. Mistakes and failures should not be considered as shameful acts. They should be looked upon as learning opportunities we have been blessed with. Knowing that, to the degree that we experience failure, we will gain the same in valuable knowledge. This should give us the confidence to embrace attempting difficult and challenging endeavors. You must be prepared to make mistakes and experience failure if you expect to grow and develop.

Consider the experience of learning to downhill snow ski. You must be willing to fall a few times if you ever desire to learn to snow ski gracefully down the hill. There are so many people who will never experience the joy and exhilarating fun associated with snow skiing because they are afraid of falling. Every success story is associated with numerous incidents of mistakes, setbacks, and failures. People succeed because they first fail and learn how to avoid those failures so they can be successful in the future. Your success depends on your ability to live with and learn from your mistakes.

Identifying the mistakes often times is the easy part. The difficult part can be admitting to the mistake and accepting the responsibility for the mistake. No one likes to be labeled as a "failure" or as a "mistake." We tend to passionately avoid such epithets. I believe attempting to avoid such labels is a primary reason people engage in making false statements and misrepresenting their actions. As humans, we believe we must show ourselves approved at all times. We believe we must display ourselves as being free of mistakes and failures to be accepted by others. So we offer falsehoods in an attempt to preserve some false image. If you know you have made a mistake, don't run away from what has happened. Accept your mistake and/or failure and immediately seek the lessons associated in the mistake. Always strive to benefit from your negative experiences. This mindset will add value to everything that you do. Sometimes success is only made possible after you have failed a few times. You should be willing to risk everything in the spirit of becoming successful. And once you become highly successful, each and every mistake you have made and failure you have experienced will have been well worth it.

Learning from experiences can deliver great levels of success if you are able to develop and master the **WACKED** approach to life:

Willingness to fail or make a mistake for the sake of succeeding,

Ability to identify failures and mistakes,

Courage to accept responsibility for failures and mistakes,

Knowledge to turn failures and mistakes into successes,

Energy to find the lessons associated with the failure or mistake, and

Determination to find the good in everything that you do.

If you put forth any effort whatsoever in any given situation; whether in your marriage, on your job, or in friendships, you have to accept the fact that your actions will supply a variety a results. Some things will work, and some things will fail. Some things will make others happy, and some things will make others upset. But to learn and grow, you must be willing to engage; and that engagement, by default, is your willingness to fail or make a mistake for the sake of success.

There are **Four Basic Types of Experiences**. One way to identify and evaluate experiences is by placing them into the following categories:

Avoidable: These types of experiences are the result of situations you knowingly and intentionally subject yourself to. An example would be you knowingly consume alcoholic beverages with the intentions of becoming intoxicated. You then drive a motor vehicle under the influence and have an accident as a result of being intoxicated.

Unavoidable: These types of experiences are the direct result of a sequence of events that evolve without your knowledge and can not be controlled by your will. An example would be you paying your bills on time, but an accounting or data entry error results in your water being turned off.

Involved: These types of experiences are generated, or at least anticipated, by your actions; and they require your participation to produce the outcome. An example would be developing heart disease as a result of you eating a diet high in fat and sodium.

Uninvolved: These types of experiences are created by the actions of others, but have a significant effect on your situation. Your efforts determine the long-term effects. An example would be an employee fails to follow your written instructions and destroys thousands of dollars of raw materials.

When a situation has not produced the desired success, there is an experience in which lessons can be gleaned. Ask yourself if the misstep, mishap, error, or misjudgment is due to conditions that were avoidable or unavoidable. Then ask yourself if you were involved or uninvolved in the circumstances that led to the misstep, mishap, error, or misjudgment. Basically there are four primary combinations: Avoidable-Involved, Avoidable-Uninvolved, Unavoidable-Involved, and Unavoidable-Uninvolved. If you can place the experience in one of the four categorical combinations, then you have identified the reason for the unfavorable situation.

Avoidable-Involved Experiences

Involved experiences are the result of significant actions on your part. These are situations you tend to create through either habits or natural acts. Natural acts and habitual acts are extremely difficult to control and even harder to change. But if you are constantly making mistakes that are avoidable, and you are fully inserted in the actions that produce your unfavorable circumstances, then you need to examine your ability to self-regulate and control your responses to given stimuli. Self-discipline and self-examination can be elusive cornerstones to success if you have never made a commitment to bringing either into fruition. But both are required if you desire to permanently vacate conditions where you make the same mistakes over and over again out of habit and natural tendencies. If you have an abusive nature and habitually mistreat people you associate with, you may be void of the necessary self-controlling attributes that can result in change drivers that will help you develop healthier habits. But if you can at least identify these traits as unfavorable and unproductive to positive relationships with other human beings, then you will be successful in completing the first step of learning from your mistakes. Avoidable-Involved experiences are normally easily identified by others, but not so easily identified by the person committing the acts because normally avoidable-involved mistakes are committed as a result of compulsive habit. Smoking cigarettes is another example of an avoidable-involved experience that is the result of a compulsive habit. While the health risks associated with cigarette smoking are widely known, the habit can be extremely challenging to abrogate.

Difficultly with change primarily involves the inability to self-discipline your intentional actions and self-control your innate or habitual impulses. So, while a person may understand the health risks associated with smoking cigarettes, the lesson is learned in vain if actions are not instituted that suggest development and growth of self-discipline and self-control. This is definitely the primary reason men engage in the act of infidelity. Men generally lack the self-discipline and self-control to avoid this relationship destroying act. Even men who have had there lives subjugated by infidelity still find difficulty in controlling the impulse in future situations. This can also be the case with company executives that become consumed by greed and an elitist nature. No CEO or CFO of a Fortune 500 company has any desire to be deprived of his or her liberty, but we find that time and time again individuals place their liberty in jeopardy because they lack self-discipline and self-control. Learning from your experiences requires self-discipline and self-control if you are to change human habits that otherwise cripple your personal development and ability to reach great achievements in life.

Refusing to accept the need to develop a greater degree of self-discipline and self-control negates one's ability to convert avoidable-involved experiences into future successes. This refusal also conveys failure to accept responsibility for your mistakes. For when you accept responsibility for a situation, that responsibility is accompanied with a commitment to making the situation either better or disappear. Learning from your experiences should cause you to avow to change your situation for the better. If you can't commit to eliminating mistakes, missteps, mishaps, errors, and weaknesses in your behavior, then you are accepting a self-imposed condition of self-stultification. Lessons in life are gifts from God that are designed to suggest in placid contrast to our failures just how we can change our lives for the better. If we fail to see many of life's lessons as gifts from God, we develop strong senses of failure and guilt. Often times this sense of failure and guilt can grow to such enormous proportions that any courage to learn from the experience and try again becomes impossible. An example of this can be illustrated in a personal experience. My first marriage was to a woman that I should have never married in the first place. Fortunately, God intervened and ensured that the marriage met its demise in a very short period of time. But the combined failure of the marriage and my refusal to accept responsibility for making the mistake of marrying my first wife in the first place initially prevented me from gleaning lessons from the experiences. As a result, I had a great sense of failure and guilt when we divorced. Additionally, the sense of failure and guilt was so large and imposing on my self-confidence that I struggled to find the courage to try again at having a healthy relationship. This feeling festered for several years. I eventually revisited the sequence of events that culminated into a situation that left me disenfranchised with romantic relationships. I identified my mistakes, accepted responsibility for my actions, and learned from the experience. At that point, growth occurred, and I matured exponentially as a young adult male. I regained the courage to engage in healthy romantic relationships once again. Refusal to receive our lessons from our experiences can prevent us from reaching proper maturation and can also exists as an insurmountable obstacle to personal growth, achievement, and high levels of success.

Avoidable-Involved experiences result from "simple" mistakes as well. I recall a day in which I was checking my daily schedule on my hand-held PDA. With the PDA in my hand, I reached into my freezer to retrieve some ice cream. Before I could react, the PDA fell from my hand to the floor. The impact rendered the PDA inoperable. A $500.00 PDA was broken because I made the simple mistake of not setting it down before reaching for a $3.00 container of ice cream. How often do you make costly mistakes because you attempt to use short-cuts or you are just too lazy to do something as you know you should? The simple avoidable-involved mistakes are often the costliest. And you want to kick yourself because they are also the easiest to avoid. They are unnecessary mistakes, but the lessons last a lifetime. I have not opened a refrigerator while either hand is occupied ever again after breaking my PDA. Simple mistakes are our most common mistakes and can provide for the greatest impact to our lives when you compare the potential gain to the actual lost. So, stop and think before you act, in every situation.

AVOIDABLE-UNINVOLVED EXPERIENCES:

Avoidable-Uninvolved experiences are the result of situations you place yourself in where you knowingly and intentionally allow your life to be subjugated by the actions of others. Life often requires involving other people in your life. Often you ask others for advice, assistance, or information. Others may also be a source of inspiration, object of affection, or measure of humanity for you. Whatever the role others may play in your life, they often provide situations and circumstances that bring with them great lessons to learn from. In many of these situations and circumstances, you do not necessarily participate in a proactive manner, but are effected by the actions of others. When I was in the military during basic training, there were many instances when the entire company would be punished because of the actions of one or a few. The idea behind that sort of group punishment is everyone in the company shares in the responsibility of ensuring everyone meets the minimum standards. The punishment becomes avoidable as long as the group is proactive in eliminating all sub-standard acts, company wide. You are uninvolved because the cause of the punishment is not directly related to acts in your commission. Often avoidable-uninvolved experiences are very prevalent in team environments. The lessons learned promote a greater team effort, thus they become extremely valuable to the long-term success of the team. Every situation has the potential of providing experiences in which we can learn from by evaluating our actions and the chain of events involved.

"Human beings, who are almost unique in having the ability to learn from the experience of others, are also remarkable for their apparent disinclination to do so."

—Douglas Adams

UNAVOIDABLE-INVOLVED AND UNAVOIDABLE-UNINVOLVED EXPERIENCES:

The word unavoidable conveys that these types of experiences can be complex. Because how can you get around something that is unavoidable? You can't, and more importantly, these are experiences God has pre-destined. The thing to remember about pre-destined experiences is that they tend to be re-occurring until you learn all the lessons associated with the experience. And the lessons can be complicated.

HOW TO HANDLE COMPLEX EXPERIENCES:

The most interesting experiences derive from complex situations, conditions, and circumstances. The more complicated the situation you find yourself in, the more patience is required to extrapolate all your lessons. You are hard pressed to identify anything worse than impulsively jumping around from idea to idea trying to find resolve for an issue you understand little to nothing about. This type of response normally results in things only getting worse.

I remember a situation with a young lady I dated years ago. She had an overhead light in her bedroom that did not work. I asked her how long the light had been inoperable. She told me the light switch had not worked in over 10 years. She said when it first started to malfunction she would simply hit the outside of the switch with her hand. She then stated that after a while that no longer worked, so she just bought a lamp for the bedroom. She knew nothing about electrical switches and how they operated. She was impatient and just went out and purchased a lamp. Being an electrician, I went and purchased a simple and cheap light switch and replaced the switch. The problem was solved. We often find ourselves in situations that require knowledge beyond our current skill set. These situations also require a great deal of patience to understand. For instance, when you become ill, you have the options of self-diagnosis or professional diagnosis. A professional doctor will subject you to a series of exams to help him or her diagnose your problem. Your doctor will have years of education and hopefully years of experience. The experience will provide patience to ensure all possible exams are conducted to assist with the diagnosis. In some cases, your doctor will even refer your case to other doctors for their professional opinions. Only by utilizing this professional approach to obtaining both an objective and subjective understanding of your illness can your doctor properly diagnose your problem and recommend the best cure. You must approach your complex situations in a similar manner.

Investigative news reporters, law enforcement investigators and scientists gather as much information in situations before making decisions. They know that in most cases they must start by discussing the circumstances with someone else. In your real life experiences, start by finding someone else to confide in concerning your circumstances. Many times we know someone who has already been where we are about to go. We are great at asking someone for advice when we are about to go on vacation to a location we know he or she has traveled on a previous occasion. But when it comes to mistakes or unchartered endeavors in everyday life, we tend not to confer with others prior to engaging the situation. As humans, it is very difficult to learn from others. For some strange reason we insist upon ramming our heads against the brick wall, even though we know it has happened to many before us without any positive gain. Engaging others in dialogue can offer you the benefit of the lesson without actually having to endure the experience. To say you have learned through the experience of another person is not a prevarication of your expressions in reference to the ultimate lessons of the experience. While I am sure that the person who shoots himself or herself in the leg with a shotgun experiences something the observer does not, the observer should be more than willing to live without the total experience. You should understand that shooting yourself in the leg is a bad thing, especially if you have just witnessed someone else shoot himself or herself.

Conferring with others also provides for revisiting the sequence of events that may have led to the unfavorable situation. Others can probe your memory in such a way that details are relived and provide insight into what you may have done that can be avoided the next time. If multiple individuals were associated with the experiences, each involved person can provide his or her perspective on the situation. This will give you a more thorough understanding of what may have given birth to the conditions you are experiencing. You must fully understand your conditions before you can fully realize all the lessons from your experiences.

While you must live life in a forward direction, learning from your experiences require you to act in a backwards direction on occasions. You must retrace your steps to understand everything that may have contributed to your situation. Until you walk backwards, you can't observe the steps that led you to where you are. Likewise, until you rethink the factors that led to the situation you are in, you can not learn all of the possible lessons in your experiences. The level of complication in the situation, condition, or circumstance, determine just how many steps you will have to retrace. Keep in mind that self-evaluation can be a difficult thing. You may get more honest results from an objective evaluator.

A PROCESS FOR SELF-EVALUATIONS:

Performing self-evaluations of your experiences can be challenging. Here are some questions that may prove helpful in your evaluations:

- Was the situation avoidable or unavoidable?

- What was the sequence of events?

- Was this a complicated or simple mistake?

- What was the original intent of your actions?

- Were the procedures correct? Did you follow the correct procedures?

- Were there early signs that a problem was developing?

- What can you do different next time the situation arises?

- Ask someone else to evaluate the experience.

- Re-visit the situation in a few days and see if your conclusions remain the same.

Evaluation of your experiences, no matter the quality of the evaluation, can not replace the practicality in the events. Always strive to live life forward stepping. Remain confident in your abilities and your understanding. When you experience mishaps, missteps, mistakes, errors, and setbacks you have to understand that these unfavorable conditions do not determine the level of your success. Your success will be determined more by how you handle a bad situation and grow from it. Never doubt your human resolve to move mountains. Each of us has this innate ability, as long as you don't allow bad situations to get the best of your spirit. Using Michael Jordan's experiences again, Michael stated that he missed over 26 game winning shots in his career. What if he did not learn from those missed game winning shots, and simply refused to take another game winning shot? He stated that he missed over 9,000 shots in his career. What if he did not learn from all those missed shots, got down on himself, and stopped playing basketball? So the most important lesson in life is that when things don't go as you plan, understand that everything will not always go your way; but you can learn from every experience and get better by evaluating the experience for important lessons. And the next time a similar situation presents itself, you will be better prepared to succeed. Aren't we all happy that Michael Jordan did not give up on himself because of a few failures or a few missed shots? No matter what happens in your life or when it happens, you can always get WACKED and learn something valuable from all your experiences; bad, good, or indifferent; and get to that place where success has only been made possible because you are willing to take the shot every time and accept the results of the shot every time.

THE NINTH CHALLENGE:

To Learn from Your Experiences:

- Accept responsibility for your actions.
- Learn to quickly identify and evaluate your misstakes.
- Realize learning begins the moment you recognize you could have done better.
- Always ask what happened and why.
- Determine if you could have avoided the situation.
- Understand the sequence of events that produced the undesired conditions.
- Determine what you can do different the next time.
- Realize that no two situations are exactly the same.
- Act to ensure failures and mistakes result in successes
- Get **WACKED!**

Challenge Ten

Understand That Greatness Has to Be Coached

"I have seen that in any great undertaking, it is not enough for a man to depend simply upon himself."

—Lone Man

To coach is to impart knowledge and skill to another person. To coach means you engage in activities that discipline, instruct, educate, school, teach, train, tutor, mentor, encourage, assist, nurture, or guide the life of another. Each one of us has been coached in life in some form or fashion. To what degree of quality and quantity varies from person to person; but our lives would not exist in the manner in which we work, play, and live without coaching. Every person enters this human experience as a totally dependent infant. As an infant, the quality of our survival is predicated on the quality of our human relationships. To a great degree we maintain a healthy degree of dependency on human relationships during our entire life span. These human relationships involve giving and receiving. This exchange of humanly activities is essentially coaching one another. This human exchange is also subconsciously constant and vehemently necessary. Human relationships are a basic human need. Without this basic need being fulfilled, we do not experience life in the normalcy in which life is designed to be experienced. In our infancy, the continuation of life would not be possible without viable and charitable care and kindness from another much more mature human. And as we mature ourselves, the quality and quantity of our existence is majorly influenced by the quality and quantity of investments others have made in our lives. The greater the quality and quantity of the investment, the greater we become. The greater the coaching, the greater we perform.

I realize absolutely none of this is a mind blowing revelation. Although, what perhaps is tantalizingly interesting is the common belief that most humans develop at some point in their lives. That common belief tends to be something of the mindset that somehow we are "self-made;" or that we are somehow where we are because of "individual self- effort" alone. I always laugh at the term "self-made millionaire" when I hear it or read it. Perhaps money, fame, and fortune have this innate ability to cause one to forget the many times another person has been an altruistic and benevolent assistance in his or her life. The mere utterance of the term "self-made" is a precipitation that is virally disrespectful to this mundane life that simply can not be lived by depending solely on oneself. Our lives would not be what they are had it not been for the mature individuals that invested heavily in our lives when we were infants, toddlers, young children, adolescents, and young adults. But why does the phenomena pervade insomuch as we get to a point where we believe we no longer require the charitable investments of others in our lives? No one, man or woman, goes about this life alone. If you attempt such, you will not experience longevity and prosperity. Whether he or she is willing to admit it or not; if he or she is a millionaire, then there has been much assisting, coaching, nurturing, mentoring, encouraging, motivating, and caring by others. For any of us to evolve into greatness; the coaching, mentoring, guidance, and teaching we receive must be enormously eleemosynary and exceedingly great in every way. And for our lives to succeed continuously and exponentially in a limitless fashion, the coaching, mentoring, guidance, and teaching must never end. When these things end, personal and professional growth ends, and your life becomes stagnant.

In his book, The Soul of a Butterfly, Muhammad Ali states, *"If I thought at age 50 as I did when I was 20 years old, I would have just wasted 30 years of my life."* Muhammad Ali's message is that the exchange of valuable investments; coaching, mentoring, guiding, and teaching that occur between humans must exist without cessation from life's beginning to life's end if we are to become the absolute best we can be. You can not waste 30 years of your life thinking you are self-made, you don't need anyone, or that you know it all. Your becoming great in your personal life is predicated on you partnering with great life-long coaches, teachers, mentors, and guiders. Your becoming a great champion in your professional life is dependent upon you developing life-long relationships with great career coaches, teachers, mentors, and guiders.

TALENT + AMBITION + VISION = GREATNESS

GREATNESS + GREAT COACHING = CHAMPIONSHIP

In the 2001-2002 and 2002-2003 National Basketball Association seasons, the New Jersey Nets franchise accomplished something the franchise had never accomplished before and has not accomplished since. The New Jersey Nets were the NBA Eastern Conference Champions both years. They lost to the Los Angeles Lakers in the NBA finals in 2002 and lost to the San Antonio Spurs in the finals in 2003. The New Jersey Nets had great player talent in the years that led up to their two consecutive Eastern Conference Championships, and they had great player talent in the years immediately following the 2002-2003 season. So what made the difference in the 2001-2002 and 2002-2003 seasons? Coaching made the difference. Player talent alone does not win championships. If it did, LeBron James would have a NBA Championship ring for every year he has been in the league. Charles Barkley, Patrick Ewing, and many other great NBA talents would not be without a NBA Championship ring. Byron Scott, the great coach of the 2001-2002 and 2002-2003 New Jersey Nets, was the difference when you look at the before and after effect of his tenure. When he left the team, Jason Kidd, Kenyon Martin, and Richard Jefferson remained with the team and remained extremely talented. Neither player has been on a team that has won a NBA Conference Championship since the departure of their professional relationship with Byron Scott. Great coaches turn great players into champions. Talent, ambition, and vision alone are not enough. Interestingly enough, when you visit the official Internet website of the National Basketball Association New Jersey Nets franchise there is no language that even remotely suggests that the success of the New Jersey Nets 2001-2002 and 2002-2003 seasons were attributed to the coaching of Byron Scott. The following are excerpts from the website:

2001-02: Nets go all the way to the NBA Finals

"The New Jersey Nets experienced a franchise-best season during their 2001-02 campaign. With a club-record 52-win season, the Nets were Atlantic Division Champions and Eastern Conference Champions and made their first appearance in the NBA Finals. The good fortune began with the trade for All-Star point guard Jason Kidd in July 2001 and escalated from there."

"Sophomore Kenyon Martin continued to show why he was a number one draft pick the season before, while rookie Richard Jefferson caught the attention of so many with his excellent play during his first year. Jason Kidd moved into the NBA's top 5 list of all-time for triple-doubles.

Kidd finished the regular season with 46."

"After defeating Indiana, Charlotte and Boston, respectively, the New Jersey Nets lost to the Los Angeles Lakers in the NBA Finals. Even with the loss, 2001-02 was a magical season and will go down in Nets history as the best ever."

2002-03: Nets make consecutive trips to NBA Finals

"For a second consecutive season, the New Jersey Nets found themselves in the NBA Finals. The Nets swept both the Boston Celtics and Detroit Pistons before falling 4-2 to the San Antonio Spurs in the Championship round."

"Despite their loss in the Finals, New Jersey celebrated another successful season, winning 49 games. Sophomore Richard Jefferson emerged as a rising young star in his starting role at small forward, while Kenyon Martin continued to be one of the most dominant power forwards in the East. The team leader, Jason Kidd, was his usual magnificent self, guiding his team all the way to the Finals."

"The team was never able to experience the impact of newly acquired Dikembe Mutombo after the center injured his wrist early on and missed the majority of the regular season. Regardless, the Nets were able to stay atop the Eastern Conference and finished just one win short of the best record in the East."

Coach Byron Scott's name is not mentioned anywhere in the passages. I understand that the talented athletes that reach stardom are the ones who sell tickets. But it is the championship teams that play to sell-out crowds in every arena they play in. The sell-out crowds are the result of the teams winning championships. The championships are the result of great talent and great coaching combined. If you separate the two, all is left is selling tickets. In your life, do you want to sell tickets to the game or do you want to win championships?

"The way a team plays as a whole determines its success. You may have the greatest bunch of individual starters in the world, but if they don't play together, the club won't be worth a dime."

—Babe Ruth

Every organization should instinctively understand that talent alone will not harness success, no matter the level of ambition, vision, and talent of the individuals. Every great company or organization has had or has a great leader that provided for the necessary coaching, teaching, mentoring, and guiding of the individual star players in the organization. Every great team, every single one of them, has had or has a great coach that coached the great ambitions and talents on the team to success and ultimate championships. The same applies with individual sport competitions like tennis or golf. The great players win championships as a result of great coaching. Even the world's greatest golfer, Tiger Woods, with all of his talent and ambition has a swing coach. If Tiger Woods understands that he needs a great coach so he can be a great champion in the sport of golf; shouldn't all organizations, teams and individuals embrace the fact that a great coach is absolutely and unequivocally necessary if great championship quality performance is the goal? Whether you are after great championship quality in your marriage, relationship with your children or siblings, employment, leadership, profession, sport competition, or other interpersonal relations; a partnership with a great coach, mentor, teacher, or guider is required. Your talent alone will not get you there. You may consider yourself a great father, mother, son, daughter, husband, wife, brother, sister, friend, co-worker, teammate, or associate; but that greatness alone will not produce a championship atmosphere in your life. Your game point averages may be high because of your talent, but your number of wins will be low because you rely on talent alone. You may have that "self-made, I don't need anyone" attitude; but your life will falter and spiral downward when your talent peaks. You can not coach yourself to the next level of success and personal performance. Honest, objectionable, and passionate self-evaluation is right next to impossible and just behind "I can't do it". Only a trained eye that observes from outside and beyond you can provide you with the honest, objectionable, and passionate coaching, mentoring, teaching, and guidance that delivers you to that place where you are a wonderful manifestation of your full potential. It is in this space where you will discover life is most abundant in every way and you are the most satisfied with your life and all that you are. This place is called Joy.

"You are never really playing an opponent. You are playing yourself, your own highest standards, and when you reach your limits; that is real joy."

—Arthur Ashe

There are many different forms of coaching. There is marriage counseling, religious guidance, professional mentoring, knowledge and skills teaching, career development, and team coaching to name a few. Your endeavor should be allowed to dictate your need. Everyone needs a spiritual leader. If you are married there is a need for some manner of guidance. Every professional should have a mentor. And if you live long enough a great relationship with a great therapist will do wonders in your life. Some decide on a Life Coach to guide them through the trials and tribulations of work, play, and life. The intent is not to advocate a particular form of coaching, just to emphasize that getting to that place called Joy is not possible without others investing in and imparting knowledge and skills to you in a great and charitable fashion. In many instances, several types of coaches, counselors, and mentors are needed in your life. For instance, my pastor provides spiritual guidance in my life in a manner that is absolutely necessary, but can not be obtained from my professional mentor. My professional mentor does not counsel me on raising my children. So you have to understand your needs so you can seek and partner with the coaching you need to satisfy all facets of your life. Just as the Hoola Hoop Paradigm teaches that you must balance a number of different guiding principles in your life simultaneously to be successful in life; you may have to engage a variety of coaching methods to address all of your needs, especially if your life is as complicated as most. In his book, *Do You!*, Russell Simmons suggests everyone should have a relationship with a Rabbi. Obviously Russell Simmons respects everyone's right to choose their own religious beliefs; but his message is that your life has to be balanced, and one of those balancing life principles is to make sure you have a spiritual guider or leader in your life that you trust and can go to in your time of need so you can extend your stay in that land called Joy. Only you, alone with your life coach, can determine what principles you need to embrace and what form of coaching you require to achieve and maintain that ever evasive balance in life.

Understand that while there are coaching forms that are heterogeneous, there are also varying methods of coaching within the multiform. When I travel, I am accompanied by the King James Bible. So I have spiritual guidance in the literary form. I can not always afford to patronize the expensive and ultra elite world of top performance coaching, but I can normally afford the audio discourse, digital videos, or books they publish. So I have professional coaching and personal development at a discount. My wife is my psycho-therapist, and my children are my great motivators. In addition to my children being my great motivators, they have become some of the greatest teachers of my life. Again, your endeavor should be allowed to dictate your need; but also be open to your needs being met in a multiplicity of manners. Avoid having only one method of satisfying your needs in life. Life is inundated with roadblocks, disconnections and interruptions. Having alternatives will serve you well. And great coaching will ensure your life has an indulgence of options along the pathways to great success and high achievement.

"Fulfilling your dreams lies in your ability to create extraordinary partnerships!"

—Tony Magee

Life is a partnership in which others make valuable investments in your development and charitable contributions to your well-being. If your life is to be extraordinary, then the partnerships you develop with others must be extraordinary. Mediocre people and people who associate with them produce only mediocre accomplishments. Extraordinary people produce extraordinary achievements. To be highly successful in your life you must think "extraordinary." Your dreams must be extraordinary. Your knowledge and skills must be extraordinary. Your partnerships must be extraordinary. Your teammates must be extraordinary. Your spouse and children must be extraordinary. Your friends must be extraordinary. Your co-workers must be extraordinary. And your coach must be extraordinary. Extraordinary does not happen by accident or by chance. I know we all know a mediocre person who accomplished an amazing feat once in his or her life. But that feat does not make the person amazing. All you observed was a mediocre person succeed at an extraordinary task once in his or her life. Extraordinary people are extraordinary every day and in every task. Extraordinary is not what you do, it is what you are. Extraordinary occurs when you develop all the investments and contributions others have made in your life into a highly principled and guided existence that incessantly extends light years beyond ordinary. In this extension, you must create an extraordinary team of partners. This extraordinary team must be guided by an extraordinary leader. When I evaluate the life and legacy of Bill Gates, the head of Microsoft, I don't valuate his life based on his level of wealth. Anyone can make money, and your goal in life should be to achieve something far greater than simply making money. I valuate the life of Bill Gates by the extraordinary team of individuals he amassed to accomplish all that they have. I valuate his life in direct proportion to not how rich he is, but rather to how many others he has made rich. That is the difference between an average person overachieving once in a while in his or her life and an extraordinary person doing extraordinary things on a daily basis. The extraordinary person is surrounded by extraordinary partners.

I recall when I worked for a company that was a manufacturer for the Aerospace and Military Armament Industry. The company had been in business since the earlier days of space exploration. At the peak, the company employed approximately 40,000 employees. When I was in their employment, the employee total was approximately 2,000. My tenure there was during the height of the Iraq and Afghanistan Wars. The company struggled to stay in business. I was perplexed to understand why a company that manufactured military armament and was a defense contractor was struggling as a company during the time of two wars. I had befriended a gentleman who had worked for the company for more than 50 years. Yes! 50 years. I posed the same question to him one day. I figured that for 50 years he had observed every situation the company had traversed. His response was the quality of leadership the company had historically employed was less than average. His statement was the company had always been a mediocre company because the leadership had always been mediocre at best. He furthered the statement by saying that a mediocre leader is void of the ability to think in an extraordinary manner, therefore the company never becomes extraordinary. My friend was absolutely correct. Mediocrity does not produce grandiosity. Great leaders are great coaches who in turn produce great environments that provides for teams and individuals achieving great levels of performance. Consider all of your top Fortune 500 companies. Those companies are where they are because of great leaders at the helm that were or are great coaches that produce great teams that achieve great levels of success.

Let's Bake Some Oatmeal Raisin Cookies

Being successful in life is like baking oatmeal raisin cookies from scratch. It all starts with a thought. You decide you want to make some oatmeal raisin cookies. Then you prepare the kitchen. You preheat the oven and retrieve all the necessary bowls, pans, utensils, and whatever you need. Then you gather the ingredients. You get the flour, yeast, vegetable oil, butter, eggs, salt, sugar, oatmeal, raisins, extract, and baking soda. Now if you have never made cookies from scratch before, you may have only an idea of what you should do with the ingredients. If you endeavor to make the cookies from scratch without someone properly guiding you through the process, the cookies could become a disaster. You have to know the right temperature for the oven. You must know the right measurement for each of the ingredients because too much or not enough of any one ingredient is going to significantly effect the taste of the cookies. You must know how long to allow the cookies to bake. You must know that the oatmeal and raisins should be soaked in water before you place them in the cookie mix so the cookies will be moist and chewy. If you don't soak the oatmeal and raisins, they will absorb too much moisture from the mix and the cookies will come out dry and brittle. So there is no way a person can make tasteful oatmeal raisin cookies from scratch without first being properly coached, mentored, taught, or guided through the process several times before a solo attempt is made. And when your oatmeal raisin cookies from scratch come out perfect and great, it is a testament to the coaching that was involved. Your life is just like those cookies. How your life evolves is predicated on the coaching you receive. Your life begins as a tiny and very dependent infant. You have absolutely no life experiences at the start of life. As you go through life you collect everything you need to be successful. At some point you have all the ingredients to be as highly successful as you desire, but you just don't know how to measure out the right amount of ingredients to make your life taste right. You don't know the correct temperature for all of your given situations, conditions, and circumstances. You may not know that some ingredients need special preparation before being added to the mix, such as the raisins and the oatmeal. There is a tremendous amount of knowledge and skill required to become extraordinarily successful, and if you are fortunate, others in your life have invested and contributed in a manner that delivers you with everything you need to have the life you want. Do not think you are self-made and don't need continuous investments and contributions from others. Get yourself the absolute best collection of life coaches possible, and your oatmeal raisin cookies will come out perfect each and every time! I know that life may appear over simplified at times and you are tempted to engage in some endeavors in a solo capacity. I know the game of golf has to appear simple to Tiger Woods at times; but allow me to state once again that if Tiger Woods understands that he needs a coach to remain at the championship level of performance in golf, you should embrace that you need one as well in your life and your endeavors. And just like Tiger Woods, be extraordinary!

THE TENTH CHALLENGE:

1. List all of your Endeavors

    - Personal Endeavors (Family, Spouse, Children, Siblings, Friends, etc.)

    - Professional Endeavors (Manager, Business Own er, CEO, Memberships, etc.)

    - Spiritual Endeavors (What Religion, Active, Inactive, etc.)

    - Career/Educational Endeavors (Current School or Position, Ultimate Goal, etc.)

    - Social Endeavors (Rotary Club, Public Boards, Commissions, etc.)

    - Team Endeavors (Sports, Academic Clubs,

2. Of all the endeavors you list, identify the endeavors in which you desire to achieve a championship level of performance.

3. List the form of coaching you will need to reach a championship level of performance in each endeavor.

4. List the method of coaching (books, seminars, personal relationships, professional consultant, etc.) you will commit your life to in each of the endeavors in which a championship level of performance is desired.

Bonus Challenge:

Learn the game of golf. If you know the game of golf, learn to play the sport better. Lower your handicap.

To master the game of golf, you have to accept and develop each of the challenges outlined in this book into principles. Golf will help demonstrate the practical implications of the princples and produce real life examples for other aspects of your life. And you will have fun playing the game!

In golf, to become great, you must:

- Discover who you are,
- Identify your ambitions,
- Align your talent with your vision,
- Develop critical thinking ability,
- Develop process patterns for success,
- Understand what works and why it works,
- Undertand what does not work and why,
- Trust in your own abilities,
- Learn from your experiences, and
- Have a great coach.

OUTRO

BECOME AS GREAT AS YOU WANT TO BE!

In many cultures, a ritualistic challenge of some sort is presented for members of the culture to undergo to prove they are ready for and worthy of the next level or position within the cultural hierarchy. Adolescent boys and girls in these cultures accept challenges to show they are ready for the rolls of manhood and womanhood, respectively. Adult men and women in some these cultures are often times required to complete challenges to determine if they are worthy of positions of authority within the culture. In some Eastern cultures birthright alone does not guarantee ascension into the higher ranks of authority and privilege. Even those of the blood lineage of royalty are often required to prove themselves in some sort of traditionally challenging manner before positions of power can be assumed. Then there are other cultures, like America, where age determines adulthood, and who your parents are can determine your level of privilege and power. Education tends to be an unfortunate forgone conclusion of a seriously antiquated socialization process. This pervasive mentality is the very beginning of a life where challenges are viewed as unfavorable. In America, there appears to be a never ending search for the "Easy" button for when things get tough or for when a comfort or a convenience in life is desired. The "American Way" tends to be a life of leisure for many. A great philosopher once referred to America as the "Hotel Culture." Americans don't desire challenges. We don't want to prove we are worthy. We want comfort and convenience. We want the unearned privilege of being able to call room service, housekeeping, and the front desk and allow someone else to complete all the challenging and inconvenient tasks associated with living so we can live a life of comfort and convenience. We use valet parking and bell services so we don't have to walk too far to get in from the outside climate or strain our physical selves by handling our own luggage. How comforting and convenient is that? And the greatest comfort and convenience of all when staying at a hotel is the services of the concierge. How many of us, when the vacation has long come to an end, strive to duplicate the convenience of the concierge in our lives, at home and at work?

So in this great American Hotel Culture you find yourself traveling the same path as 300 million others. There is no wonder the world feels crowded and everyone is marred in mediocrity. Everyone is running around searching for the "Easy" button. While everyone vehemently seeks the good life, suffering and struggling tends to be more commonplace in our lives. Many appear stuck on the large island called mediocrity looking at the distant shores of the vast land called grandiosity. The good news is grandiosity is attainable. All you have to do is be willing to give up this notion that everything should be easy. Stop looking for the "Easy" button. It does not exist. Realize that human existence was not created to be a life of comfort and convenience. You must free yourself of the Hotel Culture mentality that cripples your upward mobility. Accept the challenges of life and assume the privilege and power of that great person you are meant to be. To grow you must accept the challenges and adversity associated with your life. Extend your hands well beyond what is easily within your grasp; and the farther the reach, the greater the gain will be. Greatness will only be achieved if the challenges are great enough to deliver you to that distant shore. You alone must decide how you will live. Your commitment and determination to conquer your challenges will be vitally important to the successes of your human endeavors. The decision is yours.

Nothing in this work of literature has been definitive, simply informative. Your life will become what you make it. No book, no matter how well written and informative can transform you into something you don't have the will, commitment, and determination to become. Each of us must find our own way in this life. No work of literature is a substitute for hard work, ambition, and personal vision. Embrace what you were placed on this earth to become. Life is no fairytale. You will experience success and failure. During times of adversity and challenge, vision and determination decide the height and depth of your travels. Mere doggedness and a collection of informative books alone have never significantly served anyone's ultimate cause. Information is like a road map; you have to use the information, not just possess it, to get to where your want to go. This book is such a road map. If you use it wisely and understand that the answers you are seeking lie deep within your own soul, you will surely get to the level of greatness that you aspire to. When the front desk, room service, valet, bell, and concierge fail to make themselves available and you find yourself tested by the circumstances of your life; take comfort in the fact that adversity often is the means by which we are catapulted beyond our current conditions of stagnation and decadence. Circumstances of extreme challenge require the consolidation of our resources and the strengthening of our will. If you accept your challenges in the spirit of personal betterment, you will emerge from your challenges stronger, greater, and wiser than before. To what degree will depend heavily upon the depth of your determination, the breadth of your commitment, and the clarity of your vision. Are you up for the challenge? If so, go and become as great as you want to be!